re

Book
Famil
Faxin

P:

a

F

r

FINDING HAPPINESS

FINDING HAPPINESS
Monastic Steps for a Fulfilling Life

Christopher Jamison
Abbot of Worth

CHIVERS

British Library Cataloguing in Publication Data available

This Large Print edition published by BBC Audiobooks Ltd, Bath, 2009.
Published by arrangement with the Orion Publishing Group.

U.K. Hardcover ISBN 978 1 408 45636 1
U.K. Softcover ISBN 978 1 408 45637 8

Printed and bound in Great Britain by
CPI Antony Rowe, Chippenham and Eastbourne

Dedicated to the memory of my father who showed me how to be hopeful, to my mother who still shows me how to be faithful and to my brothers with their wives who continue to show me love.

Contents

Preface

This book is for everyone in search of happiness, so I hope that people of all religions and none will read it. The book begins by looking at ancient and modern ideas about happiness before turning to the insights of the first Christian monks and nuns. Their monastic wisdom is built upon the Christian Gospel, a faith that I delight in sharing with them, but you do not need to share this faith to enjoy their teaching as presented here. All that is needed is an enquiring mind and an open heart.

The simple idea running through the whole book is that happiness comes to us indirectly as the fruit of defeating the causes of our unhappiness. To take steps in this direction requires determination and a readiness to look at ourselves unflinchingly. The best monks and nuns of every age have possessed this determined honesty to an extraordinary degree and so they make invaluable guides on our way. I hope that some of their guidance will help you as it has helped me.

Abbot Christopher Jamison
Easter 2008

Introduction

At the start of the BBC TV series *The Monastery* I offered a simple observation which was then repeated at the beginning of each episode: 'We find that more and more nowadays, people say to us that life is too individualistic, that their life is too materialistic, that there's consumerism everywhere and that they've got more and more superficial pleasures in life and yet at a deeper level they're not happy.' This single sentence was referred to time and again by those who came to the monastery on retreat in response to the programmes. 'You were talking about me', they said.

People are searching for happiness, but not everybody knows how to find it. They speak about an ache in their hearts and disappointment with lives that on one level seem fine. This spiritual longing is becoming a common part of modern life, but many people do not know how to address it in their daily existence.

In Britain today, we are wealthier than ever and yet it seems there is a general feeling of dissatisfaction. Our society's obsession with seeking happiness through consumption and pleasure often leads to the very opposite. People are surrounded on all sides by the raging waters of modern living, a torrent so

1

great that it seems they have to jump in and go with the flow. This flow promises happiness in abundance and yet for many people the power of the flow far outstrips the strength of the happiness. All that activity and all those apparent gains give so little fulfilment.

One way of surviving the torrent of modern living other than by going with the flow is the monastic way of life. It offers not only monks but also lay people a series of stepping-stones to help us keep our footing when the current is flowing strongly. Stepping-stones are not a destination and they are not a technique, but they can help to steady our stride, giving us the confidence to keep travelling.

The stepping-stones in this book come from the Benedictine tradition, the oldest monastic way of life in the Catholic Church. One of the reasons for the durability of this tradition is that the founder, St Benedict, recognised how difficult it is to stay on the spiritual path. In the Prologue to *The Rule of St Benedict* (RB), he writes:

Do not be daunted immediately by fear and run away from the road that leads to salvation. It is bound to be narrow at the outset. But as we progress in this way of life and in faith, we shall run on the path of God's commandments, our hearts overflowing with the inexpressible delight of love. (RB, Prologue, 46–7)

Contrast this with the books about happiness in the Mind, Body and Spirit section of any large bookshop. They assume that happiness is a simple word with a simple meaning and we just need some good advice in order to achieve it. Many of them say something like 'read this book and learn a system that will make you happy'. They imply that finding happiness is a systematic process and that it is relatively easy.

The modern science of happiness offers plenty of good advice about how to achieve happiness, but remains strangely silent about how it is to be defined. The underlying assumption is that when people use the word happiness they all mean the same thing, namely, the very loose concept of 'feeling good'. A further assumption is that what makes each person feel good is a subjective opinion beyond challenge and hence happiness is irreducibly subjective. The convenient consequence of these assumptions is that these self-help books do not have to examine the harder question as to whether there is a right and a wrong definition of happiness.

When I worked as a headmaster, prospective parents would frequently say to me that above all they wanted their children to be happy. While this is a very reasonable aspiration for parents, part of me wanted to

3

challenge them and say: what do you mean by happy? Do you really want your children to 'feel good' above all else, even if they have to compromise their integrity in order to carry on 'feeling good'? Why do you not want your children to be above all decent, just and honest? I suspect that for some parents, 'happy' does indeed involve virtue, but the atmosphere around the word nowadays means that this cannot be taken for granted. It seems some people are quite prepared to be vicious rather than virtuous in order to be what they call happy.

Recently, some schools have attempted what they call 'happiness education'; yet this easily becomes health education, where health has now been expanded to include mental health. To offer mental health education in schools is a welcome development, but health should not be confused with happiness. To teach happiness does not simply mean offering healthy lifestyle advice; it means teaching that goodness and virtue are integral parts of happiness.

The Christian monastic tradition, like all classic religious and monastic traditions, sees a profound link between happiness and virtue. While there is nothing morally wrong with feeling good, it is not in itself a moral guide to right and wrong. To find such a guide, we need a wider framework. The commonly used principle 'avoid harm to others' seems to be that guide for many people, but it has the unforeseen result of allowing people to neglect the interior, spiritual world from which all our actions spring. This book offers a framework that builds on the spirituality and virtue that lies within each of us. While consequences of actions are important, the monastic framework looks into the heart and the soul of the person behind the actions. If we are to find happiness, we need to go beyond the world of simply feeling good and avoiding harm to enter the world of knowing good and doing good.

In seeking happiness, we need to keep in mind as a cautionary image the perils that await those prospecting for gold. We must beware of 'fool's gold', the natural but inauthentic mineral that looks like gold, because I believe that there is such a thing as fool's happiness. For example, some people claim that getting drunk makes them happy. But what sort of happiness is this? Is it 'fool's happiness' or real happiness? I believe that happiness is like gold and hence fakes are possible.

It is a recurring human error to identify happiness with pleasure, an error that in our day is widely promoted by our consumer culture. Monks and nuns appreciate life's simple pleasures; we often live in places of great natural beauty and we have a long tradition of producing honey, wine and cheese. Pleasure is a perfectly moral and desirable part of life. Yet such pleasures do not of themselves make a person happy; they can only be enjoyed fully if one is already happy. Tastes in pleasure vary, so one person's pleasure is another person's displeasure. If pleasure and happiness are confused, then happiness also becomes a matter of taste. By contrast, if we *distinguish* happiness from pleasure, then we can see that pleasure is indeed a matter of taste, but that happiness is not. As with gold, so with happiness careful work is needed to discern the real thing. The monastic tradition offers support in making that discernment, stepping-stones to steady our nerve as we make our choices about where to go next in search of happiness.

PART ONE

Purity of Heart

The History of Happiness

Who among you delights in life?
Psalm 34:12

Are monks happy? To say that somebody is happy can have so many different meanings: they're in love, they're drunk, they're high, they're enjoying themselves, they're exultant, they're content, they're jovial, they're lucky, they're in high spirits, they have found the perfect life. Usually the person describes his experience by saying: 'I feel good', where 'good' has an equally diverse set of meanings. Now I cannot say that monks have all or any of these experiences or that they go around feeling good the whole time. Instead, I want to make an alternative statement: I want to affirm confidently that monks are not *un*happy. This is easier to affirm because 'unhappy' seems to be a word with a narrower spectrum of meaning: unhappy simply means gloomy, forlorn and miserable.

Now I can definitely affirm that monks are not unhappy because nearly all the monks I know who are in good health (and even most of those who are unwell) do not experience life as gloomy, forlorn and miserable. They are positive people, who often carry their own and other people's burdens with impressive reserves of faith, hope and love.

In essence, the monastic tradition helps us to handle what makes us unhappy and that leads to a particular kind of happiness that is sometimes at odds with many of those diverse meanings of happiness described above.

My reluctance to describe monks as happy was shared by the father of Western monasticism, St Benedict, in his *Rule*. The title 'Rule' often misleads people into thinking that Benedict wrote a book of rules. In fact, he wrote a book of insights about Christian living, with some practical suggestions (rules) about how to put those insights into practice. The insights are still guiding people today, even though many of the rules have been adapted to local conditions as Benedict asked that they should be. At no point in his *Rule* does Benedict ever use the words 'happy' or 'happiness'. He lived his monastic life in Italy in the early sixth century, the time of the barbarian invasions of Europe, a time of extreme violence and instability, and so perhaps he wished to avoid the primitive understanding of happiness that many invading tribes brought with them. He prefers instead to speak of joy and delight, and in describing those qualities he is describing the monastic understanding of happiness.

THE ORIGINS OF MONASTIC HAPPINESS

Our monastic sense of happiness does not come out of the blue, however, and while its principal source is the Christian Gospel, the monastic tradition has built upon the Gospel with insights from ancient Greek philosophy. A good way to understand how that development happened is to look at the language people use to describe happiness.

The Latin word for happy, *felix*, also meant lucky, but even further back, *felix* came from the Greek word for fertile. In the ancient world, if you and your land were fertile, then you were lucky, and if you were lucky then you were happy. It follows then, that if luck is what makes you happy, and there is no science behind luck, then happiness is just a roll of the dice. This fatalistic sense is the primitive meaning of happiness and it is deeply seated in European culture. All the languages of Europe reflect it. In German the connection is quite explicit: the word for happiness is still the same as the word for luck: *das Gluck*.

The connection is less obvious in other languages, but a little digging soon reveals that it is there. *Happy* has its origins in the old English word *hap*, meaning luck, as still found in words like *perhaps, hapless* and *haphazard*. The French for happiness is *le bonheur*, easily mistaken for the words *bonne heure*, meaning 'good hour'; in fact, *bonheur* is a simplification of the old French *bon augure*, meaning good augury or good omen.

Fertility and luck are the first steps in the history of happiness, and alongside luck were the pagan gods, the unpredictable dispensers of fertility and wealth, and hence the dispensers of luck, whose goodwill had to be retained through ritual and sacrifice. While traces of happiness as luck remain in developed countries today—revealed, for example, in the popularity of horoscopes—most modern people do not see luck as the primary source of happiness. So how did we move beyond this primitive sense of lucky happiness?

The philosophers of ancient Greece who lived six centuries before Christ were the first people to set about freeing happiness from pure luck. They tried to see beyond the material unpredictability of life and began by looking at the constant features of nature such as mountains and rivers. Yet even as they sought permanence they perceived permanent flux: 'you can never step into the same river twice', observed Heraclitus.

The first great philosophical writer to develop a whole system of thought around stability was Plato. He arrived at Europe's first clear definition of what he considered to be the permanent aspects of life and hence of permanent happiness.

His understanding of reality took human thought into new realms, and the river provides a good illustration of this philosophy. While the water in the river is always moving and the river always changing, the idea 'river' does not change. And that unchanging idea must come from somewhere. For Plato, it came from the realm of unchanging ideas, a region where the perfect idea exists, the perfect form of everything that is. While our bodies experience change and decay, our minds know that there is something permanent beyond the material. Our minds derive such thoughts from the ideal forms of everything that exists. These forms are permanent and do not depend on human minds, although human minds can understand them. This is the origin of idealism, the belief that beyond the ceaseless change and imperfections of daily life there is a world of unchanging, perfect ideas from which every object derives its existence. While the term 'idealism' is most often used today to express belief in immutable moral ideas, Plato believed immutable ideas lie behind all aspects of life.

The existence of such a permanent, fixed world of ideas immediately has implications for the understanding of happiness; the culture of chance within which happiness had previously been imagined no longer holds sway. If life is not simply determined by a throw of the dice and the whim of the gods, if there is some permanence, if there are permanent ideas, then it becomes possible to ask a previously pointless question: how can we be happy? When life is chance, then all we can do is make offerings to the gods and hope for the best. There is no point in wasting time

14

on thinking about how to be happy. But when at least some part of human life is permanent then human happiness might be permanent as well and there emerges a whole new area of human endeavour, namely, finding happiness.

From the fifth century BC onwards, the history of European culture is driven by the search for happiness as something that humans can achieve for themselves. No longer simply fighting to survive and hold at bay the fickle elements, a growing number of people believed that they could take positive steps to be permanently happy and that they could help other people to do the same.

PLATONIC CONTEMPLATION

Plato's contribution to European culture is immense, but on our journey towards finding happiness we will concentrate on just one aspect of that contribution: his understanding of human desire. Plato believed that the fulfilment of our deepest desire leads to happiness. By speaking of desire rather than necessity Plato was giving freedom to the desirer. In the primitive view there is a chain from basic needs, to those needs fulfilled if you are lucky, to happiness. In the Platonic view another set of links emerges: the link from chosen desire, to action to fulfil that desire, to happiness when the desire is fulfilled. This self-conscious link between desire and happiness enabled people to break away from the idea of luck as the source of their happiness. Between basic need and happiness lies luck, but between chosen desire and fulfilment lies, possibly luck, but also the possibility of action. Plato and his contemporaries argued about which desires were right and which were wrong, and how they might be fulfilled. But they were agreed that the active fulfilment of desire was their key to happiness and they set about describing how to achieve it.

In essence, they said that all earthly desires are derived from the world of perfect ideas and that they all derive ultimately from the desire for perfect goodness and perfect beauty. As Plato expresses it in *The Symposium*: 'happy means possessing what is good and beautiful . . .'

He continues: 'Climbing from the love of one person to love of two; from two to the love of all physical beauty; from physical beauty to beauty in human behaviour; thence to beauty in the subjects of study; from them he finally arrives at that branch of knowledge which studies nothing but ultimate beauty. Then at last he understands what true beauty is.'

But Plato was sceptical about the value of lower pleasures which could detract from the journey to the higher happiness of goodness and beauty. People can only find happiness if they learn how to discipline their desires and regulate their lives—avoiding misguided attempts to fulfil desire. For desire has a dark potential that comes out in dreams and fantasies, in sudden obsessions and uninhibited acts. That is why for Plato, deep human desire needs to be channelled though a life of careful discipline.

This contemplation of the good and the beautiful is Platonic happiness, the first complete picture of how happiness can be achieved not by luck but by design. If the continued presence of the horoscope in our culture shows that some of us still give luck a place in our search for happiness, there is also plenty of evidence to suggest that Platonic happiness still holds sway for many people. For example, walking in beautiful countryside, attending concerts and viewing public art galleries have rarely been more popular; it's fair to assume that all those crowds at the concerts and the exhibitions believe that the contemplation of beauty will make them happy. We don't just stay at home waiting for luck to come to us, we go out to enjoy the beauty.

ARISTOTELIAN VIRTUE

Alongside this Platonic love, there is one more classical root to the monastic tradition: the classical tradition of virtue. For St Benedict, monks are people who 'delight in virtue' (RB, 7:69) and the monastic observances are 'tools for the cultivation of the virtues'. (RB, 7:3-6) Monks are happy to be virtuous and sad when they fail in virtue. Aristotle was Plato's most famous student. He shared his master's conviction that happiness was achievable and that it came from stepping beyond immediate material pleasures. Yet he was, quite literally, more down-to-earth than Plato. Where Plato looked beyond the physical realm, Aristotle looked into it. In doing so, he concluded that everything has a purpose, a final end, and that this purpose is imprinted within the thing itself. The task of the philosopher, therefore, is to discover the final end of every individual thing.

The purpose for human beings, according to Aristotle, is to be happy, but the kind of happiness we seek is also imprinted in the human soul. He argued that what distinguishes humans from other beings is reason, the rational soul, and so human happiness must be rational happiness. Rational here means acting in harmony with the final ends of all things, including the purposes of one's own body. Food and hunger provide simple examples of this: one should eat but not overeat, because the purpose of food is to nourish and give pleasure, not to make one sick and cause pain. This rational behaviour he called virtue, a way of living in harmony with nature. Hunger should tell us when to eat: to overeat is one vice, but to starve oneself or others is also a vice. The virtue is in the balance.

Aristotle knew that, while virtue was rational, it was not habitual. It can become so, however, if people are educated to it. Virtue, he said, is a disposition a person has towards making good choices, and the way we learn to make good choices is through imitation. As children, we are not virtuous, but we can be told what acts are virtuous and learn to do them until gradually they become habitual. For example, if I am brought up by a parent who is fair and consistent and teaches me to be the same, then I will grow up to be just; the virtue of justice will be natural and habitual in my dealings with other people. Such justice will bring happiness to me and to others.

Happiness for Aristotle is 'the activity of the soul expressing virtue'. So in essence where Plato sees happiness as contemplation, Aristotle sees happiness as living virtuously. Yet Aristotle, unlike Plato, concedes that luck still has a place in happiness. To call a person suffering misfortune 'happy' is a paradox he could not defend. While the luck of health and wealth is not sufficient to make us happy, Aristotle concedes that it is a necessary foundation for happiness. The skill is learning to use health and wealth virtuously.

Aristotle's virtue is as hard to achieve as

Plato's contemplation, yet it too has consistently held sway over the European imagination of happiness. In contemporary society, Aristotelian virtue is alive and well at a very practical level. We believe more than ever that children need to learn love and fairness, wisdom and good living from their parents and at school. We are told by researchers that a child's early years' experience is the key to a fulfilled adult life. In other words, the virtue of our parents and our teachers is a vital part of everybody's future happiness.

PHILOSOPHY AS A WAY OF LIVING

The ancient philosophers saw themselves as describing not just an analytic method but above all a way of living, so they devised exercises to live out their philosophy. They advocated the learning by heart of key philosophical teachings to be constantly remembered, an exercise that they called 'meditation'; they promoted self-control to live out these teachings and they devised an exercise called 'the examination of conscience' to assess how well they lived out the teachings day by day. These spiritual exercises were used by people with very different philosophies, but, long before the coming of Christianity, all agreed that such interior self-awareness was an essential component of a happy life.

From the second century AD onwards, Neoplatonism was the dominant philosophy of the Greek world, combining elements of Plato and Aristotle with philosophical exercises. Some Christian thinkers combined these Neoplatonist exercises with the way of life advocated by Christ in the Gospel. This combining of Neoplatonism and Christian faith was not without difficulties and to this day remains problematic for some Christians. It is, however, a key element in Christian monasticism. The centre for this work of combining Neoplatonism and Christianity was Alexandria, the great Egyptian port city that looked across the Mediterranean to Greece. Here Christian thinkers created a new wave of theology which had a profound influence on the early Christian monasticism that was coming to life nearby in the deserts of Egypt.

Platonic contemplation and Aristotelian virtue are key elements of monastic living. Indeed, the two are linked at the core of the monastic vision of happiness; both imply a struggle against the lower passions that lead us away from beauty and goodness. When we put the two elements together, we see that monks are people who find joy in contemplation and delight in virtue.

So if we contrast this with those meanings of happiness with which we began this chapter, we can already see a rough map of the territory we must cross. Contemporary meanings of happiness mainly involve feeling good, with the emphasis on *feeling*. Platonic contemplation involves *knowing* the good, the sense of knowing here being like that of knowing a friend rather than knowing a fact. Aristotelian virtue involves *doing* good, as in living out the virtues.

Benedict describes these experiences of knowing the good and doing good as joy and delight. For example, a monk is somebody who 'delights in virtue' (RB, 7:69). The desire to know God is described as joy when Benedict invites a monk to 'look forward to Easter with joy and spiritual longing' (RB, 49:7). So monastic steps across this territory will involve being wary of signposts that point to happiness as feeling good and will look out for paths that lead to the joy of knowing the good and the delight of doing good. To know the good and to do good we will have to struggle with all sorts of thoughts that tempt us away from the good. All the while, the siren voices of feeling good will offer us shortcuts to happiness. The monastic way of happiness as joy and delight is stronger than those voices. It offers a happiness so enduring that it can even make death happy.

A HAPPY DEATH

The words 'happy' and 'death' do not come together naturally in contemporary culture. By contrast, the Catholic tradition has prayers 'for a happy death'. So let's look at a happy death to illustrate this distinctive meaning of happiness.

Father Michael Smith was a monk of Worth and the story of his death conveys the monastic meaning of happy much more clearly than any theorising. For many years, Worth had a small community of monks living and working among the poor in Peru. Father Michael had worked there and was famous for his ability to walk over the mountains of the Andes to serve the needs of people living in remote villages: he became known as *'el gran misionero'*, 'the great missionary'. When he finally retired back to England in his eighties, he became ill and was hospitalised. He was diagnosed with inoperable, internal melanoma, the result of living for years in bright sunlight. When the diagnosis came and the consultant had explained the nature of the disease, Michael came home and I sat with him to talk it through. I explained that this disease usually affects the skin but that in rare cases it occurs internally. 'So *that*'s what's going to get me then,' he said with a tone that suggested he'd always wondered what he would die from. I said: 'Michael, you have

23

climbed many mountains in your life and now you have to climb the highest one of all.' His eyes lit up and he replied: 'Yes, I've often thought of it like that . . . and the best part a mountain is the view from the top.'

So for two months Michael climbed that mountain with great faith, and during that time his deeply spiritual qualities emerged. During his final weeks, Michael was unable to leave his room and was unable to eat; his life was reduced to the bare minimum. Having been the servant of the least, he himself now became one of the least. Yet he retained what had always been the essentials of his life: the broad grin; the prayer; the acceptance of discomfort; the concern for others, especially for Peruvians whom he still enquired about. He died as he lived. And every day he received Holy Communion in his room, with focus and great dignity. On the penultimate Sunday of his life, he was very weak and a small group of monks celebrated Mass with him in his room; at the words of consecration, 'this is my body . . . this is my blood . . .' his eyes opened very wide and his faith seemed to penetrate through the bread and wine to the Body and Blood of Christ, creating a deep sense of contemplation and communion for all of us present. During the days that followed he slowly slipped into unconsciousness and died the following week. We as a monastic community had the privilege of sharing in depth the experience of a happy death; it remains for us all a great source of inspiration and comfort.

Some of us may have had an elderly parent or relative with whom we have shared a similar experience. What is noteworthy for me is not simply that somebody on their death-bed can be grateful for having led a happy life, though that itself is a great blessing. What struck me about Father Michael's death was that the dying itself was a happy experience. In his living and in his dying, Michael knew the joy of contemplating God and the delight of living virtuously.

Clearly, dying at an advanced age, knowing that we are dying, surrounded by the loving support of friends and family, are elements of a happy death. But a happy death can take many forms. As part of our journey to find happiness, if we can appreciate what happiness means in the context of death, which, after all, is the one future experience we will all share, then we may have found an understanding of happiness that will also serve us well in life. In his *Rule*, St Benedict says that 'a monk must have death daily before his eyes'. Some may feel that this is a morbid attitude and indeed that the idea of finding happiness through thinking about death is morbid. But I believe that this approach is just the opposite; morbid means dwelling on death and being enthralled by it. I am suggesting instead that we look death in the face and in some sense conquer it by describing how it might be happy.

People diagnosed with a life-threatening illness often describe how the illness has led them to reassess their life and its priorities. This sometimes leads them to a better way of life that is simpler, giving time to what matters most in life. Without realising it, such people are fulfilling St Benedict's injunction to keep death daily before our eyes. They would be surprised if anybody called them morbid; rather, they would insist that they had found a better way to live. Keeping death daily before our eyes means thinking about how our own death could be happy. This not only enables us to accept the reality of death as part of life, it also helps us to live life now with full attention to what is truly important and so is an important part of finding happiness.

An example drawn surprisingly from the business world also illustrates how this could work for us. In the world of project management, starting at the end of a project and working backwards is called 'back planning'. When we know what the final stage looks like then we can work backwards to describe the beginnings. This approach has the advantage of generating a whole picture of what is involved; as well as telling the last step it also tells us the first step. So at the start of our journey towards finding happiness we should do some 'back planning' for a happy life, which means beginning with a description of a happy death.

Apart from the usual features of daily care and nourishment, a happy death might involve: the absence of mind-numbing pain (but the total absence of pain is not essential); the absence of anger, either because it has been passed through to acceptance or because it never occurred; a sense of communion with loved ones and with God. Ideally, it also involves a conscious awareness of what is happening so that there can be a letting go—no greedy clinging or demanding things of others. It may include a grateful looking back at life and expressions of gratitude to loved ones. This is not an exhaustive list but an intuitive one drawn from my personal experience. I suggest that we each draw up a description of our own happy death because as we do so, we will probably be discovering what a happy life involves.

A happy death as part of a life informed by contemplation and virtue describes the overall picture of our journey. This classical view of happiness can seem impossibly idealistic and excessively restrictive for people today. Freedom is integral to the modern understanding of happiness and so we must now turn to see if such a view is compatible with modern understandings of liberty and happiness.

2

Blessed are the Pure in Heart

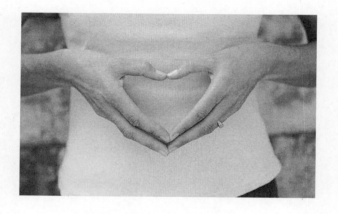

God is good to those who are pure of heart
Psalm 73:1

MONASTIC FREEDOM

'Life, liberty and the pursuit of happiness' has been the banner of modernity ever since the American Declaration of Independence coined the phrase in 1776. Freedom of choice is now considered a basic component of happiness, so that once our physical needs for food and shelter have been met, the next thing people want is freedom. This means freedom from coercion and freedom to make a series of fundamental choices: freedom to choose a partner and a home, a job and a way of life. A monk voluntarily surrenders a number of these choices, so at first glance, it seems that monks have little to teach those who live outside the monastery about happiness because we are not free. While it is true that on entering a monastery a monk relinquishes some aspects of autonomy, he does so out of a deep desire for a distinctive kind of freedom, freedom of spirit.

The monastery to which I was drawn, Worth Abbey, follows the *Rule of St Benedict*. As I explained earlier, the *Rule* is not a book of rules, but rather a book of insights and guidelines for Christian living, which are re-expressed in every age. As I reflected on the possibility of becoming a monk, it was the thought of losing my freedom that frightened me. I was afraid of losing my freedom to choose my work and of losing my free lifestyle, I was afraid of losing the right to a girlfriend and to marriage, and hardest of all I would be expected to take a vow of obedience. Eventually, hope triumphed over fear and I joined Worth Abbey as a novice.

I found my new way of life quite debilitating and the first six months left me exhausted. There is a set time and place for everything in a monastery: we pray together six times a day, we always eat together, we usually eat in silence; there is no TV and at night there is absolute silence. Above all, no matter how kind the other monks are, you are on your own. I began to suffer bouts of illness, spent Christmas in bed and was not enjoying myself; the abbot at the time nearly asked me to leave.

What I had to face up to was my own weaknesses and my own sins. The discipline of the regular life meant that nothing distracted me from my own interior world, which now came to the foreground. My fellow novices filled my horizon and so small things began to upset me. This upset could move into rage and physical illness so that my world seemed turned upside down. With skilful support from older and wiser monks, I came to see that the issues were inside me; or rather, that the issues that I could do something about were inside me. I had been led over the edge of my own competence to new territory where I had to learn from others how to move forwards. I had to admit that I could not handle my interior world on my own; I needed support and guidance. We are all instinctively afraid of the dark and I was afraid of my own darkness. But just as we can learn to overcome our fear of the physical dark so too skilful friends can help us to overcome our fear of the spiritual dark.

Easter came and something changed: I realised that the exterior framework which I found so demanding had led me to a new place where I was a freer person. I was appreciating the journey into meditation, I had fewer compulsions and I began to appreciate the diversity of my monastic brethren rather than criticising them. Above all, I saw that I needed to keep facing my own interior world and its needs. Without that awareness, I ran the risk of meeting my own needs through meeting the needs of those the monastery served. I needed to recognise my own needs and have a process for meeting them, so that I could then be truly available for others and not impose my needs on them.

I looked back and began to realise that, like a skilled guide, God was leading me through difficult mountain passes of discipline to a new world that I had not visited before. It was the world I had hoped to find by becoming a monk and God did not disappoint me. The journey over the mountains was only the first stage and there have been other difficult places to pass, such as the siren voices of pleasure, the depths of destructive emotions and the heights of pride. This book is about those places. The first step, though, was for me to realise that crossing the mountains of self-discipline is the way to that particular happiness that comes from freedom of spirit.

THE MODERN HEART

It is strange that while contemporary society places so much emphasis on external freedom, interior freedom is often given short shrift. Sometimes the way people speak about the human heart implies that in this interior world there is no freedom, that it is a fixed world that cannot be changed. With the best of intentions, we explain behaviour with phrases like 'He had a difficult childhood', or 'She's shy', or 'They're teenagers'. We can too easily take away a person's freedom by treating them as 'a case', as somebody stuck in a rut from which they cannot escape. Those with interior struggles are often held where they are by sympathy and understanding that stop short of real help to move forwards. Anger and pride, gluttony and greed, these and other feelings are not categorised by our society as disabilities yet they do prevent people from living the lives they would really like to live, either because they have a negative impact on the person experiencing them or because they have a negative impact on other people. Such thoughts are more often than not explained away as normal with a phrase such as 'that's just human nature'.

The monastic tradition believes that the interior world is a place of freedom. The monk or nun reduces their external freedom in order to concentrate on their internal freedom, the reverse of contemporary attitudes. The struggles that I experienced as a novice came from letting go of all those perfectly legitimate freedoms that people now have in our society. So why should one let them go? While the monk or nun lets them go to a radical degree, letting them go entirely is not an option for responsible lay people living in the world. So how can people benefit from this monastic emphasis on internal rather than external freedom? From discussions with lay people, the answer seems to be by recognising that the exercise of these external freedoms can become an end in itself rather than a stepping-stone towards happiness.

An example of how this works is found in the consumer society's favourite activity, shopping. 'Retail therapy' is a tongue-in-cheek phrase used to describe a particular approach to shopping. Hidden within it, however, is the germ of what can go wrong when the exercise of choice becomes an end in itself. We all need clothes, so living in a society that provides a choice of clothes at a reasonable price is a real benefit and a contribution to happiness. But when the consumer society persuades us that when we are unhappy shopping will make us happy again then life has become unbalanced. If we are unhappy, we need to look at our interior choices, not at our shopping list.

In other words, simply choosing and choosing again can distract us from that interior world which is the true source of happiness. The exercise of external freedom can become a substitute for exercising internal freedom, a displacement activity that helps people avoid some hard interior choices. Rather than finding a new job they may need to spend more time with their family, instead of a holiday they may need to face their alcohol problem. At best, external choices can alleviate the symptoms, but they don't lead to that interior delight that is the real source of happiness.

The monastic tradition retains its grip on the popular imagination precisely because of its wisdom about our inner world. There is ample evidence to show that monasticism is not an obscure or accidental development within certain religious traditions such as Catholicism or Buddhism. Rather, just as the urge to be a parent is present in all healthy adults whether or not they have children of their own, so the monastic urge is present in all spiritually healthy adults whether or not they become monks or nuns. This monastic urge is the contemplative urge, the desire to step back, be still and look inwards, the desire to find sanctuary. Learning to express this impulse is one of the steps towards finding happiness.

There are increasingly large numbers of contemporary caricatures of this, with hotels offering spas with names such as 'The Sanctuary' and even green tea adverts promising not only good digestion but also peace of mind. Finding sanctuary, however, requires a daily discipline not just a spa treatment or a consumer product. When we have created time for sanctuary in life, then the interior landscape of our life will be more clearly revealed to us, both its bright side and its dark side. To stay with what we see there requires courage to face not only the light but also the darkness of the human heart. Such contemplation involves real pain and to find contemplative happiness we must be willing to wrestle with demons. The good news is that we have sure guides to help us through this painful but rewarding process.

During the twentieth century, the monastic traditions of Asia became widely known in Europe and America. The Buddhist and Hindu traditions seemed to provide guidance for this inner journey that was not found in ordinary people's experience of Christianity.

More recently shamanistic teaching has become popular, resulting in courses offering an eclectic mix put together by Western practitioners. But Western culture has spiritual guidance available much closer to home. The Christian monastic tradition integrates the inner journey with the teachings of Christ, and that is one of its great achievements. Jesus, the Son of God who wrestled with the demons in the desert, is the centre of the Christian monastic project.

PURITY OF HEART

One Sunday morning in 271 AD, in a small village near Alexandria, a twenty-year-old man called Antony was attending church. He heard read out the gospel passage that said: 'If you would be perfect, sell your possessions and give to the poor and you will have treasure in heaven. Then come, follow me.' He took this to heart and left everything to live in the inhospitable world of the Egyptian desert, there to contemplate God. In that barren world, his life was fruitful. He became the first to describe the art of 'fighting your demons', famously declaring that we should expect temptation right up to our last breath. St Antony of Egypt died at the legendary age of 105, and his desert life is one of the foundations of Christian monasticism.

The first Christian monks and nuns were inspired by the example of St Antony. They lived in the deserts of the Middle East in the fourth and fifth centuries and became known as the desert fathers and mothers, living in loose associations and gradually founding more structured monasteries. The wisest of them acquired the title abba for men and amma for women, meaning father and mother respectively, which later become abbot and abbess. Their sayings and stories will accompany us as we take our steps along the road. They did not use the language of freedom, a language that has come to dominate modern discourse. Their central concern was purity of heart, which we might describe as freedom of spirit.

Purity has overtones that make many people feel uncomfortable. It is connected to the word puritan and so is associated with the negative approach to life conveyed by that term. In a sexual context, purity is used to mean virginity, a meaning strengthened by a modern campaign for sexual abstinence among teenagers that says that it is promoting purity, with no adjective to say that by this they mean sexual purity. The Christian monastic teaching about purity of heart cannot be identifled with either of these limited meanings. The purity of heart described by the first monks is founded on people's innate capacity for goodness and sees sexuality as one among several areas of life requiring careful practice in order to allow that goodness to flourish.

For the first Christian monks and nuns, the notion of purity and impurity is a general one, not one confined to a single area of life. In using those terms, they are describing the conflicting tendencies to right and wrong found in the human heart. To achieve purity of heart is for them the immediate goal that inspires them to heroic efforts in resisting evil and embracing goodness. So the term 'pure' here is not associated with innocence and there is no sense of returning to some pristine state. Purity is not something inherited at birth and then lost; purity of heart is a hard-won quality of somebody focused on leaving behind negative thoughts and embracing only the good. When we have achieved this focus as a permanent state of mind, then we have achieved purity of heart.

The desert fathers compared purity of heart to the target that a javelin thrower aimed at in the ancient games; a small target may be difficult to hit but it can be done and the effort required draws out the best from the thrower. So purity of heart describes the condition of human beings at their best, when the human capacity for love finds complete expression devoid of any selfish thought. To arrive at this state of being is demanding because human beings are continually tempted to behave selfishly, but the example of many saints shows that it can be done.

The first step towards achieving purity of heart is to recognise the realities of the human psyche. The desert fathers and mothers discovered authentic insights about the interior world by living in extreme conditions of solitude and simplicity. They were as realistic as modern psychologists about the passions and struggles of the interior world, but they never wavered in their conviction that they were free to choose an interior life that was more integrated than the one they currently experienced. Just as we now send business managers on outward bound courses in remote and wild locations in order to discover more about themselves, so too the first monks and nuns went into the deserts of the Middle East to discover themselves and God. Once there, the first interior realities that they noticed were their thoughts and in particular those thoughts that unsettled them and tried to persuade them to give up their interior journey. These negative thoughts are present in all human hearts and most people half recognise them but avoid really facing them, fearing such powerful inner realities. The early monks and nuns turned and faced them with unflinching honesty and courage, free from all distractions and escapes.

They noticed that these thoughts came in a pattern that was common to all of them. They observed that they are eight in number: the first three are thoughts about the body: gluttony, lust and greed; the next three are thoughts in the heart and mind, namely, anger, sadness and *acedia*; finally, two in the soul, vanity and pride. These are the Eight Thoughts and they provide the framework of our search for happiness. We will look at most of them in the original order, except that we will begin with *acedia* because it is so destructive in contemporary culture. *Acedia* is a Latin word (pronounced ah-see-de-ya, as in encyclopaedia) which means 'carelessness' and which in this context can be translated as spiritual carelessness or apathy. The next chapter will look at it in more detail.

To face the Eight Thoughts and to overcome them lies at the heart of the monastic way to find happiness. The presence of these thoughts does not mean that a person has done something wrong; they are present in everybody's life. The only difference is between those who have noticed that these thoughts need to be wrestled with and those who have not.

Our monastic steps will also help us to explore the opposite virtues of the Eight Thoughts. Three virtues in the body: moderation, chaste love and generosity. Three virtues in the heart and mind: gentleness, gladness and spiritual awareness. Two virtues in the soul: magnanimity and humility. Human nature is such that in order to live out these delightful virtues we will need first of all to understand the Eight Thoughts.

The Eight Thoughts have the potential to damage our well-being, they throw us off balance and lead us away from happiness. They come from within us and yet sometimes they seem to be bigger than we are and so they are described as attacking us from without. That is why the desert fathers and mothers also called them demons. Anger, for instance, is a thought but it is also a demon that can grip people in such a way that they commit terrible acts that seem completely out of character. Some legal systems (interestingly, not stiff-upper-lip British law) recognise that people who commit crimes of passion are not in possession of themselves, so there are much-reduced penalties for a crime such as killing on the spot the man you find in bed with your wife. Such systems recognise that we can be possessed by something other than our normal self, possessed by demonic rage, or quite simply possessed by a demon.

The desert fathers and mothers lived in a culture that had a strong belief in the reality of the Devil as a personal force of evil in the world, and they saw the demons as his servants, sent to entice people away from virtuous living. According to this theology, however, the Devil is not simply a force equal and opposite to God, because while God can act directly on people when He wills (through the grace of God) the Devil can only act indirectly. He acts through the vices. When people freely choose to turn the Eight Thoughts into actions then vice is indulged and the demons have their entry into the soul; to choose to enact negative thoughts is a free choice that leads to vice and in extreme cases to actions that seem to be by a man possessed. So the demons are always working to persuade us to turn our thoughts into vices, but we are completely free to choose not to do so.

On our journey towards happiness, our principal guide to understanding the Eight Thoughts and their demons will be John Cassian. Born in Eastern Europe around 360 AD, he became a monk in his twenties and went to live in several monasteries in the Middle East. Cassian is notable as the first person who set about systematically writing down the teachings of the desert fathers and mothers. This record is found in the *Institutes* he wrote for the monks and nuns of the monasteries he founded and in the *Conferences* he gave to the monks living on the islands of Lerins, off Cannes in the South of France. All quotations from Cassian come from those two works. Cassian died by 440 and Benedict was born in 480, but he was Benedict's guide and inspiration. It is through Cassian that the teachings of the desert fathers and mothers of the Middle East found their way into Europe and into our culture. I smile at the thought that a fourth-century monk speaking just a ferry-ride away from Cannes and its film festival was the first person to introduce Europeans to the world of inner demons, demons all too often invoked by film-stars to excuse their addictions.

So we do not have to share the demonology of the fourth century to believe that not only do people experience negative thoughts that cause them to act badly, but that also in some cases their vices literally seem to possess them. But just as the demons can be freely embraced, so too they can be freely renounced. For Cassian, constant awareness of the interior life was the royal road to purity of heart: but the demons constantly distract us from this state of mind. To overcome this distraction, Cassian advises us to pray the psalm verse: 'O God, come to my assistance, O Lord, make haste to help me.' The constant repetition of this simple prayer is his way of freely choosing purity of heart at every moment of the day.

Some may be tempted to see in this whole attitude a very old-fashioned approach that has been dislodged by modern psychology. Yet one of the most effective movements of modern times which has liberated millions of people from vicious behaviour is based on precisely this approach. The phrase that is used to describe one of the most widespread modern addictions is 'the demon drink', showing how this image of the demons is still part of our way of thinking. Alcoholics Anonymous offers a programme to become free from this demon drink. The process involves the Twelve Steps derived from the personal experience of the earliest members. The heart of the programme is the middle third of the Twelve Steps, Steps 4-7. They are expressed as follows:

4   *We made a searching and fearless moral inventory of ourselves.*
5   *We admitted to God, to ourselves and to another human being the exact nature of our wrongs.*
6   *We were entirely ready to have God remove all these defects of character.*
7   *We humbly asked Him to remove our shortcomings.*

Freely choosing to drink to excess is now replaced by freely asking God to save us.

The Twelve Steps of AA mirror in a remarkable way the lived experience of the desert. The difference is that the desert tradition sees this approach as applying to all the demons not just to alcohol. We enter our inner world, name its demons and then ask for help to contain them. In a way, then, this book will apply the Twelve Steps to the whole of life and in doing so will take a different direction to many contemporary books on happiness.

There is no advice here, for example, about setting goals or knowing our own strengths. These are indeed important aspects of life and others have written about them at length. Rather, just as the Twelve Steps of AA are described as a personal recovery programme, the monastic steps are a personal recovery programme for our interior life. For reasons ranging from the decline of religion to the rise of consumerism, our society is in danger of losing its soul; these steps are offered as a personal soul-recovery programme. The assumption is that if we find our soul and rescue it from the demons, then we will be on the way to inner freedom and happiness. The monastic steps help us to take the spiritual life seriously and as an indirect result we come to interior joy and delight. But the steps needed to recover true interior freedom are not easy. Our consolation is that the early monks and nuns knew this, even having to remind each other not to be too hard on the ordinary people who came to them for guidance.

This compassionate approach is beautifully illustrated in the monastic discussion of alcohol. In his *Rule*, one of St Benedict's most endearing chapters is on the subject of wine. Benedict lived in the late fifth and early sixth centuries, so the desert fathers, who represented a past golden age of monastic observance were his heroes. 'We read', says Benedict, 'that monks should not drink wine', a view that he has inherited from the desert tradition. However, Benedict always balances idealism with realism, and so he goes on to say: 'but since monks nowadays cannot be convinced of this, let us at least agree to drink moderately' (RB, 40:6). And he specifies half a pint a day. Benedict's humane understanding is an encouragement as we set out to examine the steps that the monastic tradition offers us to handle the thoughts and demons that lie between us and the happiness of a pure heart.

PART TWO

Eight Thoughts

FIRST THOUGHT:

Acedia

The whole wide world will remember
Psalm 22:27

In 2004 a MORI poll commissioned by the BBC asked over a thousand Britons if they had ever committed any of the Seven Deadly Sins, namely, pride, envy, anger, sloth, greed, gluttony and lust. Top of the list was anger, committed by nearly 80 per cent, with all the other sins being committed by well over half of those interviewed. But when asked 'Which is Britain's deadliest sin?' they mostly ignored the traditional seven and went for cruelty and adultery as the two worst. When asked which of the deadly sins they enjoyed, the easy winner was lust followed by gluttony. In the subsequent reporting of the survey, the list of Seven Deadly Sins was treated as a bit of a joke. Some writers and actors were asked for comments on the deadly sins and said frankly they couldn't see what was wrong with most of them. 'Whatever you're doing, with pride you never drop below a certain standard.' 'Anger isn't a sin; it's good to let off steam.' 'Sloth is doing nothing. How can doing nothing get such a bad press?' The fundamental attitude was 'where's the harm in a bit of pride or sloth?' In a world where 'avoiding harm to others' is the overriding moral rule, the Seven Deadly Sins seem to have had their day.

Yet looking more closely at the responses to the opinion poll, it is surprising that those who saw cruelty as the top sin did not connect it to anger as the source of cruelty and did not see lust as the source of adultery. People today see wrongdoing solely in terms of outcomes. The private sphere is mine to command exactly as I like and in the public sphere I have only to avoid harm to others. In so far as they are seen as key actions that harm others then the Seven Deadly Sins are indeed unhelpful. They are only useful when seen as describing the principal human tendencies that lead people away from living well towards harmful actions. In other words, their usefulness is dependent on a belief that spiritual awareness is a vital dimension of human life and that without such self-awareness there is no happiness. The Seven Deadly Sins were never intended as a guide to harmful actions, but as a guide to the roots of harmful actions; when viewed in that way, their insights continue to challenge us to greater personal honesty about our innermost thoughts.

EIGHT THOUGHTS OR SEVEN SINS?

The framework of this book is the Eight Thoughts from which the Seven Deadly Sins are derived and the change from one list to the other is significant. The transformation began with Pope Gregory the Great in the sixth century. He was a monk of St Andrew's Abbey in Rome and he would have been familiar with the monastic tradition of Cassian. But he wanted a guide for lay people and so he set about amending Cassian's list. Further revisions followed in later centuries to arrive at the list of what are known formally as the Capital Sins, capital meaning the head or source of all our sins, colloquially called the Deadly Sins.

Gregory began this process by removing from the list *acedia* as he considered it something that mainly afflicted monks and nuns. The disappearance of *acedia* from ordinary people's vocabulary deprived Western culture of the ability to name an important feature of the spiritual life, namely, loss of enthusiasm for the spiritual life itself. While the word has disappeared, the reality of spiritual carelessness is strongly present in our culture.

KNOW THYSELF

The purpose of all such lists of thoughts or sins is to provide a framework within which people can develop their self-awareness. Self-awareness here has a particular meaning that we need to distinguish from introspection; introspection is only looking at me, whereas self-awareness involves considering how I interact with the world around me. Self-awareness is attentiveness to my way of relating to people and things. In particular, it involves understanding how my outlook affects the way I see the world and how it affects the world itself. This self-aware life does not accept that there is a private world of introspection and a public world of action. It insists that my interaction with the world includes my attitudes as well as my actions. This approach refuses to accept the modern belief that something is good so long as it does no harm to others. My own inner world is a place that can do harm or do good not only to myself but to other people as well. Simply being angry, for example, is bad for me and bad for those who have to deal with me; the vibrations of my anger affect others even if I never do anything bad. So self-awareness here means an awareness of my place in the world.

Without such self-awareness, the inner life of human beings will lead them to do wrong. Legislation and policing alone will not prevent public harm to others nor will telling people that harm to others is bad. We need people to work on their self-awareness and we need to teach children to do this from an early age. If we want to protect the environment, then we ask people to contain their greed. If we want to reduce violence, we help people to contain their anger, and so on. We have to enable each person to live out the discipline of self-awareness not only for personal happiness but also for society's happiness.

This takes us straight back to the opening chapter of this book. The fundamental insight shared by the ancient philosophers and by Christ is that an interior discipline of thoughts is needed. The only way to avoid bad actions and promote happiness is to go deeper than the actions themselves and to train our thoughts.

This deep human insight is expressed by Jesus with imaginative force in the Sermon on the Mount (Matthew's Gospel 5: 21-22 and 27-28).

> You were told 'do not kill' and that if you do kill you will answer for it before the court. But I say anyone who is angry with another person will answer for it before the court.
>
> You were told 'do not commit adultery' but I say that if you look at a person lustfully, you have already committed adultery with them in your heart.

This is not Jesus simply creating impossibly high standards; he is saying that anger and lust are the origins of murder and adultery so get a hold of them before it is too late. As a society, we seem to have forgotten this very simple insight.

57

ACEDIA: THE FORGOTTEN DEADLY SIN

One way of viewing our current situation in Western society is that we have suffered a catastrophic loss of understanding of the need for self-awareness leading to widespread acedia. Until the modern era, the Church and especially its religious orders provided a constant reminder to ordinary people of their need to examine their conscience every day and to reflect deeply on their way of life. The Church provided a series of exercises, some simple and some complex, to enable people of all kinds to live a self-aware life. At its worst, this provoked unhelpful guilt, which we will examine more closely later. At its best, these spiritual exercises enabled people to remain self-aware. Pre-modern European societies were often ignorant, poor and sometimes cruel, but they had a strong sense of the vital importance of the interior world of each human being. That interior world was the resource that enabled them to survive the horrors of their age.

The interior world of human beings is a mixture of irrational and rational forces. The spiritual exercise of reason was the ancient and monastic response to this world, with daily reflection on the workings of my innermost soul; from such exercises flowed the solutions to life's challenges and temptations. By contrast, in our culture, we are brought up without explicit and systematic spiritual formation, being informed that we can do and think what we like provided that we don't harm others. Spiritual practices such as meditation are considered purely optional extras for an eccentric few and so we are subtly led to understand that the spiritual struggle is not worth the effort. While we want music with 'soul' and condemn 'soulless' bureaucrats, we have created a culture of spiritual carelessness that neglects the disciplined life of the soul. This state of mind is often accompanied by statements such as 'I have no time for that sort of thing', where having no time means both not having enough hours in the day and not having the inclination.

In the list of the Eight Thoughts, *acedia* comes in sixth place, and while we will look at the other thoughts in their original order, *acedia* is the first demon to be addressed here. The reason for this rearrangement is that spiritual carelessness seems to me to underlie much contemporary unhappiness in Western culture. The word is no longer used not because the reality is obsolete but because we have stopped noticing it. We are too busy to be spiritually self-aware and our children grow up in a culture that suffers from collective *acedia*. *Acedia* has established itself so well that it is now part of modernity.

A parallel can be drawn with the world of

medicine. Before the discovery of germs, hygiene was not considered essential so that many deaths were caused by infections that nobody could see. Once the existence of germs had been identifled, physical hygiene became rigorous and lives were saved. Similarly, the cause of much unhappiness lies hidden from view but is truly present. Our demons are unseen thoughts that make us unhappy and spiritual hygiene is as necessary as medical hygiene if these diseases of the soul are to be healed. But we are a spiritually unhygienic society. While we know that we must find time to brush our teeth, to visit the doctor and to take exercise, we have no such shared conviction about the need for spiritual exercises.

ACEDIA, MONKS AND MARRIED COUPLES

Even monks and nuns can experience the temptation to forget about the spiritual life. In one ancient collection of stories about the desert fathers and mothers, the very first story begins with a surprising statement about the most famous monk of all. 'When the holy Abba Antony lived in the desert he was beset by *acedia*.' Towards the end of that same collection Amma Syncletica offers the insight that '*acedia* is full of mockery'. Our society is 'full of mockery' towards those who insist on the reality of the soul and its essential disciplines, disciplines which have been preserved almost uniquely by the best of the world's religious traditions but which are scorned by increasingly strident atheist commentators.

It comes as quite a surprise to lay people to discover that monks and nuns really are haunted by the thought that this whole spiritual project is a waste of time. It is easy to see the whole monastic enterprise as ridiculous, especially if you live inside it. This is obviously not a temptation for keen new entrants to the monastery, but it is for those who have spent a good part of their life on the monastic path, the ones of whom you might least expect it. From my experience as abbot, I know that a monk can be overwhelmed by spiritual exhaustion; is it worth persevering, they wonder. The thought grows that this way of life isn't valid for me any longer, that my companions are not right and that I should be doing something else, not wasting my life here. As the discipline of the monastic life becomes distasteful, so it is slowly worn away: less prayer, less self-awareness and a growing rejection of the life of the community. Alongside this is often found the impulse to replace spiritual exercises with more and more good deeds. In my experience, it is particularly difficult to get monks to recognise that this is what is happening to them, since they too are affected by the cultural assumption that sees outcomes as overriding all other considerations. This is a subtle and persuasive demon not only for modern society but also for modern monks.

Unlike other thoughts such as gluttony and lust, this thought is not easy to discern. According to Cassian, the first quality of this thought is that 'it makes a person horrified at where he is . . . disdainful and contemptuous of the brothers as being careless and unspiritual'. The monk then inevitably becomes slothful and 'complains and sighs, lamenting that he is bereft and void of all spiritual gain in that place'. In essence, this first quality of spiritual apathy is a deep sense of being in the wrong place surrounded by the wrong people doing the wrong things.

The second quality flows inevitably from the first. The monk decides that he will perish if he stays here any longer so he must leave and go to far-off places where everything is better. These two features of disdain for the familiar and a desire to give up are at the heart of *acedia* and they appear to bear some similarity to what modern psychoanalysis calls a mid-life crisis.

There are similarities with the experience of couples who have been married for a number of years. The all too common story of a long-established marriage where a spouse leaves home for somebody else often has overtones of *acedia*. The husband or the wife becomes 'disdainful' of their spouse who is seen as 'careless and unspiritual'. So they must leave for somebody better. The *acedia* of marriage can be a very real trial for the couple, and to name it as such may be a helpful starting-point to enable the relationship to grow beyond it.

The monastic tradition identifies the demon of *acedia* not so much with a phase of life as with a time of day. The midday hour is the moment when *acedia* shows itself, leading to the nickname, 'the noonday demon'. In the middle of the day, the monk is exhausted and hungry, as if he had been working hard all day long when in fact he has been doing nothing of the sort. He looks at the midday sun and convinces himself that it isn't moving.

Next, he starts complaining that none of the other monks ever come to visit him. He is so disengaged from the spiritual life that he craves either a visitor or sleep as the only things he wants. Since nobody is coming to visit him, he'd better go and visit them. 'Those relatives should be looked after, and he should hasten to bring his greetings to them more often; it would be a great and pious work to make frequent visits to that religious woman . . .' Cassian gets into quite a comic vein as he describes in more and more detail the reasons why the monk should leave the monastery and go elsewhere to do good to all sorts of needy people.

Cassian concludes this section by describing how the monk substitutes outward movement for inner perseverance. 'And so the unhappy soul . . . gets in the habit of finding consolation in the face of this onslaught [of *acedia*] by visiting a brother, although the soul will be all the more painfully vulnerable not long after having used this remedy as a stopgap.' Here too there are parallels with family life. Many people immerse themselves in their work and are good at it, only to return home to personal situations that they find too painful to face. The danger is that hard work and even good works become painkillers that fix the symptoms but leave the sickness untreated. Recognising this very modern *acedia* can be a liberation leading to a better way forward.

So is Cassian against doing good to others? By no means, but he does want us to be careful about our motives. If the agitated visiting of others is a 'remedy' for being unhappy back at home, then he describes it as an avoidance mechanism. 'Experience proves that an onslaught of *acedia* must not be avoided by flight but overcome through resistance.' If we are going to be happy, we will need to learn to face up to *acedia* rather than just avoiding it.

THE REMEDY FOR ACEDIA

Acedia involves filling up my inner space with everything other than the desire to recognise and overcome the other seven thoughts. We have an interior space, our soul, which is a space that we can fill with endless distractions and avoidance mechanisms. If we can remove some of the avoidance mechanisms, then our self-awareness will grow quite naturally. Gossip and idle curiosity are top of the list of things to avoid; these activities waste our time, distracting us from more generous and thoughtful conversation or reading. Celebrity news magazines would be a good example of this; they do no apparent external harm, but are a complete waste of interior time and space. So cut out reading rubbish and allow reading time to become spiritual reading. This is the first remedy for spiritual apathy; to read spiritual books and reflect on what they are saying about our own lives. A good book can help us to stay focused on what matters, free from distraction. In the Christian monastic tradition pride of place is given to reading the Bible prayerfully, a reading style called *lectio divina*. This slow reading has been compared to eating: firstly, bite off the words by simply reading them; then chew them, that is, repeat them again and again in meditation; then swallow by making those words into a prayer and finally enjoy the flavour of the words in silent contemplation. Such meditative reading is a real antidote to *acedia* and there are some wonderful modern aids around to help in this area, ranging from monthly Bible reading guides to podcast meditations.

As well as gossip, Cassian highlights envy as an avoidance mechanism. Envy tells us to stop facing the challenges of our present life and to live in some future fantasy; it is a subtle form of *acedia*. We want what others have and hence we are no longer content to accept where we are and what we have. Such envy drives a large part of our consumer culture, and consumer envy can so absorb our interest that there is no room for anything else. Spiritual desire is drowned out by the siren voices of the market-place. To keep our spiritual desire alive in the face of envy we must come back to the present moment and the way to live in the present moment is to pray.

Prayer can take many different forms but the key point is that it must be disciplined and sustained, the very features that *acedia* tells us are pointless. In brief, monastic prayer is the carving out of sacred time and space dedicated to rejoicing in the goodness of God and repenting of the thoughts that impede that goodness in my life. So try to create a sacred space at home, maybe something as simple as an icon, and build a time of quiet into the day, a time to visit the sacred space. If you have young children, bring them with you to share in this special time. Some parents tell me that the children are better than they are at always insisting on this time of prayer. Others find a train journey to work can be a time of spiritual reading and prayer; the regularity of the journey safeguards this sacred time. So each of us needs to find a sacred time and space that becomes as integral to life as brushing our teeth.

This is the bedrock that helps us grow in self-awareness. Spiritual reading and prayer help us to recognise our demons while also helping us to contain them. As we spend time persevering in prayer and meditation, we become aware of the interior movements of the whole self, body, mind and soul. Our culture implies that indulging the Seven Deadly Sins is the way to happiness; more food, more things and more sex, combined with personal aggression and vanity, are the way to happiness. This is the message hitting us day by day. The good news is that most people in their heart of hearts know this message is a lie, but many lack the means to live out an alternative. This spiritually careless culture does not have to run our lives, however, and helping people to overcome our culture's endemic *acedia* is one of the purposes of this book.

If *acedia* is spiritual carelessness, then overcoming it is achieved by taking seriously the other seven thoughts and looking honestly at their workings in my life. We begin by looking at the way we handle our thoughts about food, something that is basic not only to physical life but also to spiritual life.

SECOND THOUGHT:
Gluttony

*Bring forth food from the earth
and wine to cheer people's hearts*
Psalm 104:14

When they went to live a simple life in the silent sanctuary of the desert, the first thing the desert fathers and mothers noticed was that food was one of the main items looming large in their minds. So they would not have been surprised to know that it remains a constant preoccupation for human beings today, whether we are thinking about eating too much or too little, or worrying about the effect it will have on our physical appearance. Food is as basic as life gets and even though the developed world has no difficulty feeding itself, disorderly thoughts about food are a common source of unhappiness in this world of plenty. Controlling those thoughts is a key step on the spiritual journey.

FOR STARTERS

Never has so much food been as easily and quickly available as it is today, and yet Western culture suffers from both too much eating and too little, from obesity and anorexia, or other eating disorders. Although food is physical, the use of it begins with a thought—my mind says 'I fancy a cup of coffee'—but we often do not notice that thought; we just set about making the coffee and drinking it. So eating is an activity that involves the mind, the will and the body, and the monastic tradition sees in it the starting-point for learning how to live with spiritual attentiveness. This attentiveness is a person's ability to be aware of what they are thinking, what they are choosing and what they are doing; a complete awareness of their mind, their will and their body; an awareness that after long years of monastic living eventually becomes habitual and permanent. This attentiveness is at the heart of the interior freedom we looked at in the previous chapter, and is a vital part of the monastic tradition of happiness. The monk or nun must grow in consciousness of all aspects of life, and they must therefore begin with a new appreciation of thoughts and actions regarding food. 'Food thoughts' need to be mastered as the very first step along the path of human fulfilment. If we can't be aware of something as simple as food we have no chance of addressing the fiercer and more complex demons such as anger and pride.

The Bible itself reflects this in its very structure: food comes first. While the Genesis story of creation is an obvious starting-point for the Bible, the first Bible story in which humans are the actors is built around eating. God tells Adam: 'You may freely eat of every tree of the garden but of the tree of the knowledge of good and evil you shall not eat; for in the day that you eat of it you shall die' (Genesis 2:16-17). Adam and Eve are led by the serpent to ignore that command and they eat the forbidden fruit. The serpent's line of argument is to insist that God has misled them: 'You will not die. For God knows that when you eat of it . . . you will be like God, knowing good and evil' (Genesis 3:4-5).

The structure of this episode is important: firstly, people are offered a right and a wrong way to eat; then a demonic force suggests ignoring that injunction, on the grounds that the distinction is erroneous and finally somebody eats badly with dire consequences. While Adam and Eve's basic sin is the sin of pride, nevertheless, the means by which they express their pride is eating. The process by which they come to eat badly is one that we can still see happening today, not only as it applies to food but also in a whole range of human activities where people are misled into thinking that their choices won't have consequences: amassing consumer goods, seeking excitement to keep boredom at bay, the obsession with celebrity. All these apparently harmless activities stir up the demons of greed, spiritual apathy and vanity, and they are not good for the soul. Doubtless Adam and Eve said about the forbidden fruit what people say about these thoughts and actions: what harm is it doing? The serpent's line of argument still has a powerful effect in people's lives.

At the other end of the Bible, food issues

mark the beginning of Jesus's active ministry. When Jesus heard a voice from heaven speaking to him at his baptism and was led into the desert by the Spirit, it was there that he came to realise that he had a unique role in proclaiming the coming Kingdom of God. The uniqueness was Jesus's insight that the Kingdom would come in hidden ways *before* it came in power and glory: it would come first through the weak and the poor, through love and forgiveness. Or to put it another way: for Jesus, the power and the glory of God would come in the love and the forgiveness, a conviction that Jesus lived out faithfully in his own final crucifixion and resurrection—events his disciples believed to be the definitive coming of God's Kingdom.

The relevance of this to our reflections on food is that Jesus came to these insights while he was praying and fasting in the desert after being baptised by his cousin John the Baptist. His self-awareness through fasting was an essential background to this prayer and discernment. His temptations in the desert came at the end of forty days of fasting, 'after which he was hungry', both Matthew and Luke tell us. So the devil's first temptation comes to Jesus via the food demon who says, 'If you are the Son of God, command these stones to become loaves of bread.' Cassian reflects that, having trapped the first Adam with food, the devil then tries the same trick on Jesus, the

Second Adam. But this time the devil can make no headway. And so too with the temptation to greed in which the devil promises Jesus all the wealth of the nations, and the temptation to pride in which he invites Jesus to throw himself from the Temple roof. Cassian notes that each of the demons that succeeded in Adam failed in Jesus.

Just as food plays a central role in the beginning of Jesus's ministry so too it plays a central role in concluding his ministry among his disciples, when he eats the last supper with them. Yet this food is not only a conclusion but also a new beginning, as Jesus chooses food as the means by which his followers are to remember him in future. 'Now as they were eating, Jesus took bread, and blessed, and broke it, and gave it to his disciples. "Take, eat; this is my body." And he took a cup, he gave it to them, saying, "Drink of it, all of you; for this is my blood of the covenant, which is poured out for many for the forgiveness of sins"' (Matthew 26:26-28). This eating and drinking continues to this day as the central act of Christian worship and remembrance. As St Paul says: 'as often as you eat this bread and drink the cup, you proclaim the Lord's death until he comes' (1 Corinthians 11:26).

The early monks and nuns were very aware of the role of food in scripture, especially at the beginning of God's work. So they believed that for them too, a correct approach to food

75

must mark the beginning of the spiritual life.

THE HAPPY MEDIUM

So how should we handle food thoughts in order to begin? According to Cassian, 'It is an old saying that extremes meet. For the extreme of fasting comes to the same end as overeating does.' Overeating is the same today as it was then, and while excessive fasting is not the equivalent of having an eating disorder, nevertheless there is common ground. Cassian's insight about extremes comes from a series of talks he gave on the subject of discretion, known traditionally as the mother of all the virtues. Discretion enables people to find the happy medium, that place of balance between extremes. This is particularly necessary with food, where our thoughts and demons are always tempting us to extremes.

Women sometimes have different experiences of food thoughts to men, so it is interesting to hear a desert mother's opinion. Amma Syncletica notices that 'there is a fasting that is determined by the devil and his disciples practise it. So how are we to distinguish between the divine asceticism and the demonic tyranny? Clearly through its quality of balance. Always use a single rule of fasting. Do not fast four or five days and break it the following day with any amount of food.

In truth lack of proportion always corrupts.'

The monastic tradition values fasting as a key step towards spiritual fulfilment, but monastic fasting does not mean starving ourselves. Eating modestly and only at set times is the monastic way of fasting and its aim is to prevent food thoughts dominating our lives. Monastic fasting involves more intense periods of food reduction such as Lent, but never to the point where the fasting leads to *more* rather than less thoughts about food. People can become obsessive either about gorging themselves or about starving themselves or about moving from one extreme to the other. As we reflect on our food thoughts, we might consider how to spend less time thinking about food and simply enjoying modest but regular eating.

To make this fasting sustainable over a lifetime, Cassian invites his monks to eat at the right time and to eat what is offered, whether they feel like it or not: 'We should be on guard lest, out of a desire to coddle our bodies, we slip into harmful waywardness and presume to indulge in food before the prescribed time and to exceed the appointed measure; so we should accept the refreshment and sleep at the proper time, even if it is unpleasant.' This of course presupposes that there is a structure to the monks' day that includes regular meal times, and that they have learnt some sense of discretion in eating.

FAST

At this point, monastic living comes up against the modern culture of fast-food outlets in the high street combined with food on the run at home. The monastic fast meets fast food. Food is necessary for humans, a fact recognised both by the monastic tradition and by modern food culture. But the similarity ends there. The fast-food culture tempts us to ceaseless food consumption, and food on the run at home invites us to do our own thing without reference to others. Both tend to be impulsive activities undertaken without much thought. The monastic tradition, by contrast, wants us to be aware of eating and of not eating, choosing both thoughtfully. This awareness about eating and fasting involves several factors. Firstly, each of us needs to be aware that eating is a significant activity in life; so we need to take a moment to review how we approach it. Do we eat too much or too little? Or do we fluctuate between those two extremes? Do we treat eating as just refuelling? To help answer those questions, here are some monastic responses.

The question of how much food constitutes neither too much nor too little was one frequently asked by the desert monks and nuns. The answer Cassian gives is that each day a monk should eat two loaves of bread each weighing a pound. That is a lot of bread, and Cassian contrasts it with the meagre diet of fruit and vegetables that some monks tried to live on; fruit and veg are not plentiful in the desert and meat was rarely available there. So Cassian did not want his monks to feel hungry after they had eaten at the set times and a pound of bread twice a day would certainly achieve that, even if it is in a way that is not very healthy by modern standards.

St Benedict as usual takes the strict desert tradition and adapts it. He begins by saying that he is wary of regulating how much another person should eat; he would much rather not do that because he recognises how much people's needs vary. Since he is pressed to do it, however, he says that the main community meal of the day should include two cooked dishes to choose from, so that a monk may find a dish that is to his liking. As in most ascetic traditions, Benedict says that monks should abstain from the meat of four-footed animals, so presumably other meat is acceptable, possibly because it is cheaper, less substantial and less likely to provoke overeating. The aim of all this is to ensure that no monk leaves the table feeling hungry. The danger of this generous food regime, as Benedict notes, is that a monk can unthinkingly eat too much. In another one of his very human moments he says that 'above all overindulgence is to be avoided lest a monk experience indigestion' (RB, 39:7). Although an older version translates the original Latin with the memorable phrase 'it is unfitting for a monk to be surprised by a surfeit'.

Moreover, if after the meal a monk asks for something that he has already refused during the meal, he may not have it. Eating for Benedict is not an indulgence, it is a duty and an act of obedience, so eating what is offered when it is offered is not only self-interested but also selfless. Those of us who live in monasteries know that allowing somebody else to choose our food day after day, even decent food, is a considerable discipline of the spirit. We really do just get on and eat it, simply letting go of thoughts about eating something tastier, which is what Benedict wants.

Benedict also wants the common meals to be taken together in silence while one monk reads and others serve those eating. Here we arrive at the heart of a deep approach to food which sees that a shared meal is about much more than just food. This monastic practice combines thoughtful eating, listening and serving. In families similar principles can be promoted through family meals, and groups of friends or students sometimes agree to share a meal together once a week to promote friendship and common values. The shared meal is a repository of many important ideals.

FEAST

The monastic tradition, along with the whole Catholic tradition, values a shared meal as part of celebrating special events in the life of the Church. The Feast Day is still a lively part of Catholic culture. Special food as part of celebration is a human impulse to which monks and nuns have contributed richly over the centuries, whether making good wine or special cheese. And the monk-pharmacist has for centuries been providing herbal remedies for all kinds of sickness; monks have long believed that the right kind of food can heal.

Food is also part of another core monastic value: hospitality. Cassian asks that a monk keep some of his bread until mid-afternoon so that if a guest comes he will have something to share with them. Benedict creates a special part of the monastery, the guest house, as an exclusive unit to welcome guests, including a separate kitchen. The usual rules of eating may be waived in order that the abbot might share food with a guest. So hospitality is a principle that must affect the way we organise our eating; we must always leave room in our food arrangements for the unexpected guest, for in the visitor it is Christ himself who is received, says St Benedict. In this vision of hospitality, we see clearly how our food arrangements can have built into them a sense of the other, especially a sense of the other who is in need of food. A desert father's story with a difference illustrates this point.

Modern-day Egypt is a place where the ancient desert tradition is still surprisingly alive, as an American Benedictine monk, Fr Mark Gruber, discovered in the 1980s. He went there to do research for his doctorate in anthropology about the Coptic people of Egypt. For this, he had to travel to the Coptic monasteries of Upper Egypt and the lower Nile valley, which are on the same sites as the ancient hermitages and monasteries of the fourth and fifth centuries. There he met the desert tradition in its primitive form, before it was translated into European culture by St Benedict. He encountered not only the monks of the desert but also the desert nomads, with their remarkable tradition of hospitality that is reflected in so many bible stories. When exploring the desert one day, Fr Mark's jeep broke down so he set out on foot to seek help and came across a Bedouin camp. There the Bedouin not only washed his hands and feet with their precious water, but they insisted he take food. The bread he was given was the typical nomadic bread which they bake in large quantities when near a water source, with a hard, thick crust to preserve it; once opened in the heat of the desert, it dries out quickly and so the whole loaf has to be eaten. Even as Fr Mark was eating the first loaf, the father of the tent-dwellers broke open a second. Fr Mark thanked him and nibbled at it, saying that he was full, so could the Bedouin now help him with the jeep problem. The third loaf was opened and he was urged to eat. He forced down the third loaf and nibbled at the fourth, complaining that he could eat no more. 'When my protests became louder and more forceful', recounts Fr Mark, 'the head of the house did something really incredible! He took one loaf after another from all that were lying before me—all of the bread of his family—and broke each one open in front of my face! The gesture was unmistakable. He wanted me to know that he had withheld from me nothing, that he had put before me everything at his disposal.' The way people handle food is a good barometer not only of their inner world but also of their generosity to others. Such generous hospitality brings happiness not only to the guest but also to the host. Eating good food is a pleasure, but sharing good food with guests brings delight. Here we see food used in a way that opens life into virtue, so that happiness is found in the dimension beyond pleasure.

ALL CONSUMING

So the monastic awareness about food involves reviewing our whole approach to eating, not just reviewing our diet; we need to understand that this approach is a fundamental aspect of spiritual living. Then it asks us to make sure there is enough quantity and choice of food to prevent us feeling hungry but always avoiding excess. It invites us to eat only at appointed times and it says that we should accept the food we receive at the hands of other people. Finally, it says that we should offer food to others, both in serving at table and as part of our hospitality to those who visit us. Building this approach into life today requires a very conscious set of decisions. The tradition of grace before meals is one simple way of building self-awareness about eating into our lives. Militating against this is a strongly consumerised food industry—a force pulling in the opposite direction to the monastic tradition of eating.

The consumer process is the commercial procedure by which items are made into commodities. To use a product like wheat flour as an example: in a non-consumer society, such as pre-eighteenth-century agricultural England, people grew wheat that they either sold directly at the local market, or took to the local miller to make into flour that he would then sell to a merchant or keep for his personal consumption. By contrast, today wheat from one country is sold to a wholesaler in another country, then to a flour-milling plant, then sold on to be made into bread and packaged by somebody else; finally it is sold on to a consumer who is now at a great distance from the original producer. The final retail outlet, usually a supermarket or a fast-food chain, puts pressure on the potential buyer to consume more and more. This is the kind of consumer society that dominates modern Western culture.

It has become common place to denounce this system because of some of its intensive production methods; yet viewed independently of those methods, in itself this system strikes me as having real merit because it has done so much to eradicate hunger in the developed world. Those on limited incomes have access to more, and cheaper, food, food supplies are regular and public health has improved as a result.

From a monastic perspective, the main drawback with this system is that it drives away awareness about food and concentrates on selling it to us as a product for rapid gratification rather than as necessary human fuel to be used as part of spiritual living. Children in particular are subjected to this through marketing techniques that combine powerful media images with food products: such as plastic figures from films packaged inside breakfast cereals, fast-food outlets selling burgers with names derived from movies, confectionery placed at check-out tills to encourage children's pester power to force parents into undesired purchases.

Of course, one of the stunning features of our society's consumerised industries is their extraordinary ability to consumerise those who criticise them. A symbolic example of this occurred in 1997, the 150th anniversary of the publication of the Communist Manifesto; a book-store chain responded by selling copies of the text in a new special edition that they piled high and sold cheap. Once the enemy of big business, Marx himself had now been turned into big business.

The same has happened to the food industry: concerns about too many fatty foods have led to 'lite' products; complaints about farming methods have led to a boom in organic products, while compassion for poor coffee farmers in the developing world getting a poor price for their coffee beans has led to the Fair Trade movement, which in turn led to supermarkets producing their own fairly traded coffee.In other words, the food industry can take on board criticism and turn it into a marketing advantage.

I suspect, however, that the monastic critique is one that will remain resistant to such a transformation by the industry. Awareness, the avoidance of impulse eating, choosing to eat enough but never more than is needed, always keeping in mind other people as being part of one's eating experience: these are difficult steps for people in our modern, consumer world to take. But through facing these food thoughts we have started on the path to fulfilment, because learning these skills will help us to tackle the other demons that stand in the way of finding happiness.

THIRD THOUGHT:
Lust

*Kindness and faithful love pursue
me every day of my life*
Psalm 23:6

MATTER-OF-FACT

The search for happiness can be baffling. For all the insights that wise and brilliant people have come up with over many centuries, the nagging suspicion remains that happiness is pretty simple and pretty basic. All the sophistication of Roman civilisation could not dissuade some Romans from retaining a decidedly unsophisticated understanding of happiness. Nowhere is this more clearly demonstrated than on the wall of the bakery in the ruined city of Pompeii. Amid all the refined splendours of that great city, the phrase *hic habitat felicitas* (here dwells happiness) is carved around the simple outline of an erect penis.

The desert fathers and mothers had a similarly down-to-earth approach to sex and, while they did not think sexual indulgence was the path to happiness, they did know that dealing with sex was a key step along that path. Some of John Cassian's writings about sex are so explicit that the Victorian era did not know what to do with them. His advice about monks' problems with nocturnal fantasies and wet dreams was so explicit that the nineteenth-century translators of his works left those sections in Latin; they were only translated into English in the 1980s (though into French much earlier).

The first monks and nuns were under no illusions about sex; they recognised it as the most powerful and pervasive of all the thoughts, the demon that attacked them most violently. They did not, however, see it as the most lethal thought; that role is reserved for the last two demons, pride and vanity, whose presence is often hidden from the one who is gripped by them and hence those demons are more dangerous. By contrast, the person experiencing sexual thoughts is usually only too aware of what they are experiencing. In working to master our thoughts about sex we can therefore be encouraged by the desert fathers: everybody has sexual thoughts and one of the aims of the monastic tradition is to help us to direct them rather than be directed by them, to enable us to be free from such thoughts dominating our lives. This is about freedom from sexual thoughts that lead us into destructive rather than constructive actions: good people can destroy relationships by sexual infidelity; we can destroy our integrity through sexual obsession; and we can find ourselves seduced by another person's sexual advances in a way that threatens our wellbeing. So understanding our own sexuality and containing the sexual demon that can grip any of us is a key step on the journey towards finding happiness.

Before looking at what monks say about sex,

let us reflect on some contemporary attitudes towards it. In Britain, the second half of the twentieth century saw the widespread availability of artificial contraception and the disappearance of Christian sexual morality as the norm; taken together, these two changes have led to a whole new way of understanding sexuality. Detached from procreation and even detached from ongoing relationships, sex could become different things to different people; it could be for love, for recreation, for procreation, for marriage, for union between people of the same gender. In this area of life, more than perhaps any other, people now demand freedom of choice.

Freedom can have many meanings, as we have already seen. Sadly, the meaning of sexual freedom today is often reduced to sexual licence; for many people, sexual freedom means sexual activity as and when we want it. The effects of this are often disturbing, especially in the lives of the young. The age of first sexual intercourse moved from 20 for men and 21 for women in the 1950s to 16 for both by the mid-1990s. The movement of first serious sexual activity from an adult setting to a school setting in such a short space of time is astonishing. One result is that social institutions are now scrambling to set limits on young teenage sexual activity by a variety of contradictory means: some are offering more information about sex, others are demanding abstinence from it, one group encourages easier abortion while another resists abortion altogether, and some legislators suggest lower age limits and others want higher age limits.

This is the context within which we live our sexual lives today and within which we read the wisdom of the desert about sexual thoughts. As a result, contemporary attitudes and those of the desert monks can seem light years apart. Yet the desert fathers and mothers lived during the decline of the Roman Empire, a time notorious for sexual excesses. They made their choices not against a background of Victorian modesty but from within a culture that, as illustrated on the walls of Pompeii, was sexually uninhibited. Their insights therefore spring from a sexual climate that shared some similarities with our own. The insights offered here come from people of integrity who had a very bodily view of sexuality and who saw sexual integrity in terms of a struggle for chastity. How to be faithful in a sexual relationship is an enduring concern for every generation and, as we will see, chastity properly understood is still a vital ingredient in sexual fidelity.

DIFFERENT KINDS OF SEX, DIFFERENT KINDS OF CHASTITY

The desert fathers and mothers noticed first of all that there are three kinds of sexual activity: sexual intercourse with another person, sexual self-stimulation and sexual thoughts. Any of these three can dominate somebody, and the desert fathers were unsurprised by the power of each and all of them.

Their methods to achieve freedom from this domination are based on a science of the human body that we do not share, but their psychological and spiritual insights are still valuable. The desert fathers and mothers, in line with the understanding of their era, thought that the proximity of the sexual organs to the stomach meant that overeating stimulated sexual activity. Hence they connected fasting and sexual abstinence. While the physiology may be wrong, the psychology is still helpful. The self-awareness about food that we explored in the previous chapter is a good first step towards sexual self-awareness. Food and drink are often the favoured preludes to sexual activity: think of the cliché of the annual office party, where free food and drink lead not infrequently to allegations of sexual harassment; or the regrettable one-night stand that is blamed on both parties having too much to drink.

Contemporary experience bears out the monastic insight that there is a connection between uncontrolled eating and drinking and loss of sexual control.

So self-awareness about food is a good introduction to the way the desert fathers approach sexual thoughts. While they opted for the monastic, celibate way themselves, their attitude can be of help to anybody who wishes to contain sexual thoughts that trouble them. Now somebody may say that they have sexual thoughts which don't trouble them; quite the opposite, they say they enjoy them. The desert tradition invites us to challenge ourselves, to grow in awareness of the nature of our sexual thoughts. In the same way that we are invited to examine our food thoughts, for example, checking a tendency to compulsive snacking, so too we are invited to consider whether our indulgence of sexual thoughts is healthy. The word healthy here needs clarifying: the desert fathers and mothers were not concerned about obesity and sexually transmitted disease, important as those issues are nowadays. They were concerned with spiritual health; namely, how to avoid indulging thoughts that hindered the process of soul-making and growth in virtue. Just as we need to be spiritually attentive about our approaches to food so we should be equally attentive to our sexual behaviour, building up our awareness not only of exterior lifestyle but of our interior world as well.

Once we have reached this starting-point, the next step involves being aware of the choices that we can make as regards sexual activity. A person's sexuality invites them to make choices in three areas of life: sexual activity, sexual status and sexual integrity.

As regards sexual activity, we can choose sexual abstinence, which means no genital activity, or we can choose to be active; this choice is not a permanent one and it may vary from time to time; for example, a person who becomes HIV+ may have been sexually active but then chooses to stop all sexual contact.

The second choice is about status, where we can choose to be single, married or celibate (i.e. committed for life to being single). The status of long-term partners has also become common in recent decades and, while the Christian tradition does not sanction this status, it is nevertheless a sexual status choice made by increasing numbers of people.

The third and final choice is whether or not we choose to be chaste, but let me clarify the meaning of chastity. Celibacy for the monk or nun means a lifelong commitment to live without a sexual partner. Sometimes the word chastity is used to mean exactly the same as celibacy and so confusion arises. There is a wider meaning of chastity, however, and that is the one being used here. To be chaste in this sense is to live out our chosen sexual status with integrity, being faithful to a marriage partner for example. The temptation to live unchastely is as great for a married person as for an unmarried one. Chastity is a virtue that can be lived out by everybody not just by those committed to lifelong celibacy but, as a virtue, chastity takes time to develop until it is a habitual disposition of heart and mind. Sadly, the social customs and commercial practices of Western culture do not support the development of chastity as a virtue; while grateful for removing sexual repression, many people now wonder how we allowed ourselves to lose a whole tradition of sexual self-discipline as well.

The choices we make in the three areas of sexual activity, sexual status and sexual integrity are interconnected. For example, a married couple may choose to exercise sexual abstinence temporarily or they may have it imposed on them by illness. This distinction of three areas of choice enables the challenge of the desert tradition to become clear. The desert fathers chose abstinence as regards sexual activity, they chose to be celibate as regards their status and they aspired to be chaste. The most vital choice is the last one, the option for chastity, and it is in this choice that everybody can imitate them. According to the Christian tradition and the tradition of all the world's classic religions, the goal for true human fulfilment in sexual matters is chastity, remaining faithful to our chosen path.

The monastic tradition obviously deals primarily with celibates, people committed to a lifetime with no sexual partner. This particular engagement is very difficult to comprehend for people in Western culture today; in a world of unparalleled sexual freedom, we might choose to be single for a time, but why would any sane person choose to be celibate for life? The force of this question is of course strengthened by the terrible abuse of minors by clergy that has come to light in recent years. These men had singularly failed to be mindful about their sex thoughts and a scandalously inadequate system of management and accountability failed to recognise the terrible damage they were doing to young people. The failure of these men as celibates does not, in my opinion, invalidate celibacy nor does it invalidate the monastic insights about sexuality. Rather, this appalling chapter of recent church history reinforces my wish to understand how the desert fathers and mothers as pioneers of Christian celibacy understood and lived out this demanding vocation in a way that won awestruck approval from their contemporaries, both from ordinary people and from political leaders. Indeed, it was precisely this admiration that led to priests being asked to adopt celibacy as their status.

The Catholic Church has chosen to insist that priests in the West must be celibate (unless they are convert clergy from other churches). While celibacy is essential to the monastic life, it is not part of the definition of the priestly life. There are many reasons for a celibate priesthood, but it is important here simply to understand the difference between the celibate discipline placed upon priests and the essential nature of celibacy for monks and nuns.

So returning to the question as to why anybody would want to be celibate: the reason is out of love. Only love is strong enough to carry somebody through the celibate life. Love of God's call to be a monk or nun, love of God's call to serve people as a celibate and the love of God which we experience when we respond to this vocation. The word monk derives from the word *'monachos'*, meaning one alone (the word monarch comes from the same root), and so by definition a monk is celibate. After my difficult experience of being a novice, I have experienced a real love for the monastic way of life; I love being a monk, its prayer and its community life, and I love the opportunities for service to others that it constantly offers me. Being celibate is an integral part of that; while all that I do could be done by married people, nevertheless, being celibate adds a distinctive quality to the way I do them. Put simply, they are all that I have and I depend on them, not on family or sexual intimacy. In the end, being celibate is not simply a reminder of my dependence on God, it is the actual living out of that total dependence. And that is why monks and nuns have constantly to check that they are not seeking their fulfilment outside this celibate life and hence compromising the radical love of God which sustains them.

This love inspires us as celibates to meet the very real challenges of sex thoughts, and in doing so to find delight within the monastic tradition. The same can, I believe, be true for those who are not monks or priests. Married people want to maintain the integrity of their relationship, and love empowers them to face the temptations to be unfaithful that may strike them. Single people, especially the young, also need to find a loving motivation for setting out on the path of chastity. Perhaps the first love is a healthy self-respect and a real desire to do nothing that will diminish our sense of ourselves: 'love thy neighbour as thyself' implies that we love ourselves, meaning we have a sense of our own value in the eyes of God. I say in the eyes of God, because all too often people have a very low opinion of themselves. For example, if you ask a group of people, especially, in my experience, young people, to list their faults they will write at length; ask them to write down their virtues and they stare at a blank piece of paper for a long time before daring to write anything. The sense that God loves us is important in order for us to have a healthy self-esteem that can be combined with real humility: we know that we get things wrong but God's love sustains us.

To this healthy sense of self can be added a love of the community to which we belong and a respect for—as opposed to a fear of—its insights about relationships, sex and marriage: respect that the traditional boundaries placed around sexual activity has something positive to offer us. Of course, this presupposes a healthy family and community background, something that seems to be increasingly rare in our diverse society, which now has a range of family experiences that stretches from forced marriage on the one hand to sexual licence on the other. Such negative realities should not make us lose sight of the many benefits found in the traditional wisdom about relationships and marriage.

Inspired by love, then, the monastic tradition offers certain disciplines to the person wishing to live out the freedom of chastity (be it as a single, married or celibate person). Some disciplines are only for celibates, but there is much that it is of help to all. While they may contradict some contemporary views, they are presented here as complementary to the many valuable insights of the behavioural sciences.

FACING THE DEMON

At the start of his discussion on chastity, Cassian asks whether sexual desire can be completely extinguished. That question would not occur to most people today; they may want sexual desire to be contained, but they would not suggest that it should be eliminated altogether. Yet Cassian's response is as much about how to contain sexual desire as it is about how to extinguish it, so those who are single, married or celibate can all learn from it. While Cassian was writing about chastity for celibates what follows applies to chastity for everybody, where chastity means being faithful to our sexual status.

Cassian states that the curtailment of sexual desire is possible yet no matter what steps a person takes, in the end, perfect chastity is the gift of God. He is particularly exercised by how much a monk is responsible for his own nocturnal sexual fantasies accompanied by sexual arousal and emissions. He even discusses the effects of a full bladder and of past memories on such arousal. He concludes that monks should recognise that such things are not obstacles to prayer but rather encouragements to more fervent prayer. He says that this is why sexual desire is good for us; it makes us realise that we are dependent on God and so encourages us to be more faithful to Christ's teaching in our lives and in our prayer. So there is a double effect from this realisation that we cannot become chaste other than as a gift of God: we are both more zealous in living virtuously and we are more faithful in our devotion to God. In a comparison that shocks us today, he says that eunuchs are lukewarm in the pursuit of virtue because they believe themselves free from threats to their chastity. He quotes Proverbs: 'a person in sorrow labours for himself and forcibly prevents his own ruin'. So our sorrow at our lack of chastity is a good spur to greater virtue and faith. So while the desert tradition says that sexual desire needs to be contained or even extinguished, it also says that sexual desire is good for us.

A short episode about a desert mother illustrates the point. It was related about Amma Sarah that for thirteen years she waged war against the demon of fornication. She never prayed that the warfare should cease, but she said: 'O God, give me strength.'

Cassian did offer some suggestions for a technique that would help to achieve perfect chastity: if we put aside useless conversation, anger and material concerns, if we eat simply and sleep for four hours (remember the desert heat usually meant early rising and a siesta), and if we believe that not our efforts but God alone can grant us the gift of chastity, then within six months we will know that chastity is not impossible for us. Note that he does not say that after six months we will be completely chaste, but that we will know that it is a possibility for us.

Central to handling this area of life is the desert tradition of revealing thoughts, not just sexual thoughts but all the thoughts and demons that trouble a person. A monk simply tells another monk, usually older and wiser, all the thoughts that are going through his mind. The older monk's function is to listen but not to offer advice. In other words, the act of speaking out the thoughts is the purpose of the exercise; it is not psychoanalysis. It was a favourite saying of the desert fathers that the demons love nothing so much as a thought that has not been revealed. This desert practice of sharing thoughts would later evolve into the Catholic practice of Confession, known nowadays as the Sacrament of Reconciliation. This takes us back to the Twelve Steps of Alcoholics Anonymous: Step 4 is to conduct a fearless moral inventory and Step 5 is to admit the exact nature of our wrongs not only to ourselves and God but to another person. In the area of sexual thoughts and actions this is particularly demanding. And in secular society, where Confession is unknown, who is there to whom I can speak my sexual thoughts? Therapists and counsellors are of course one option, but most people just want a listening ear and there have been some interesting experiments recently. During the Edinburgh Festival 2007, for example, Catholic priests simply offered Confession 'on the high street' to anybody who wanted to talk, not just Catholics wanting absolution of their sins. Many hundreds of people availed themselves of this service.

There is a story that tells of a desert father who crossed the line of listening and gave bad advice. One day, a young monk came to an elder to confess his thoughts: 'I am obsessed with sexual thoughts', said the young man and proceeded to describe them. The older monk was horrified and told him so, adding that anybody with such terrible thoughts was unfit to be monk. So the younger monk went away sad, having determined to leave the monastery.

Another monk came across the dejected young monk and asked him what the matter was. 'I am leaving the monastery,' said the young monk, and proceeded to explain why. His companion was horrified by the reaction of the old monk and prayed that the Lord would that night send the demon of lust to the old monk. And the Lord did so and the old monk was overwhelmed by sexual desire. Realising that he was being punished for his hasty judgement on a brother, next morning the old monk rushed to ask the brother's forgiveness and begged him to stay.

As well as listening, the father with whom

the monk shared his thoughts might also offer a word or text from the Bible: this is the origin of the saying 'a word to live by'. The text was offered just as a doctor offers a prescription today: having listened to the symptoms, the doctor of the soul offers a medicine for healing, a word from God that the monk can use day by day to help his spiritual health. This is a part of living with mind and heart alert so that self-awareness does not desert us; the sacred phrase is repeated to keep the mind focused on the choices we want to make.

Another part of the way to make progress towards chastity is to notice the thought coming and to take evasive action. This is often described as dashing the thought on the rock of Christ. One of the more unsavoury parts of the Psalms comes in Psalm 137 when by the rivers of Babylon the Jews in exile sat and wept, remembering Zion. In their anger at their plight they wished that their captors' children would be dashed against the rocks. That violent text had to have a Christian meaning for the desert fathers because of their belief that the whole Bible is of value. So they saw in this a metaphor in which the children are the beginnings of bad thoughts and Christ is the rock against which to hurl them to their death. Not an appealing modern image but one that shows a shocking seriousness about our freedom to entertain or to destroy the thoughts that come to us. We can learn a mental discipline to walk away from them by saying a prayer, by taking a walk or by simply doing something practical. The most favoured practical activity for monks to defeat the demons is hospitality: in other words, an act of love towards somebody else.

LOVE CHASTITY

For modern readers, perfect chastity can seem unattractively daunting rather than inspiringly desirable. And this highlights an interesting point: do we really *want* to be completely chaste? In his Rule, St Benedict mentions chastity on only one occasion; he simply says 'love chastity'. I once participated in a workshop for abbots in America and the monk leading the workshop dealing with this issue simply said: 'Please will all those who love chastity raise their hand.' If he had said all those who love food or art or beauty raise their hand we would all have done so like a shot, but when he unexpectedly asked us did we love chastity, we all hesitated. I suspect we rarely think of chastity as something to love and instead we see it as a burden. If we can rediscover chastity as a privilege to aspire to and a gift to seek, then the context of our struggle for chastity changes completely.

Whereas sex may be about love but may also be about selfishness, by contrast chastity is always about love: a living out of one's marriage vows for love of one's spouse; a faithful observance of celibacy out of love of Christ's call to be a monk or nun. All this contributes to that most fundamental desire of the monastic tradition, the desire for purity of heart. The pure in heart see God and the most persistent attacks on purity of heart come from sexual thoughts; but no matter how persistent, these thoughts are not as deadly as the demons of the soul, pride and vanity. The first three material thoughts all originate in emotional upsurges that we call gluttony, lust and greed. The desert tradition offers ways of sustaining our freedom of spirit during those surging moments when our bodies are tempted to let go of our awareness and our integrity. Finally, then, we look at fostering that freedom as regards the last of the material thoughts: greed.

FOURTH THOUGHT:
Greed

My happiness is in none of the sacred spirits of the earth

Psalm 16:3

The first three thoughts of the desert fathers and mothers all deal with the material side of life, but the two we have looked at so far, gluttony and lust, both originate inside the body: they are the body's internal urges. By contrast, the final material thought, greed, traditionally known as avarice, deals with what presses upon us from outside, namely our attraction to money and things. As Cassian noted, greed is not a natural, internal desire like food and sex, it invades our bodies by slow degrees and has more far-reaching and disastrous effects than either gluttony or lust.

Those far-reaching consequences are both personal and communal. It is a striking feature of many happiness self-help books that they deal solely with personal rather than communal happiness. In this chapter, I want to offer some monastic steps towards handling both personal and communal greed. In taking these steps we are not only contributing to our own happiness, but to that of others as well.

OUR GREEDY CULTURE

Greed lies at the heart of many contemporary political and social problems. Industries are the wealth creators of our culture which have polluted and continue to pollute the environment; but we are loath to pay the price of restraining or abolishing them. Our Western way of life demands that we take natural resources from poor countries as cheaply as possible; we avoid paying a fair price and so poor farmers remain poor. Our Western financial institutions have become caught up in a web of loans to poor countries of such complexity that poor people are now massively in debt to rich people; greed on all sides has fuelled the nightmare of Third World Debt. We are caught up in a culture that has brought great benefits to many people through industrialisation and globalisation, but we are also aware that those benefits have been bought at a terrible price, a price that has been both financially too low and environmentally too high. We are a greedy culture and neither communism nor capitalism has succeeded in curbing the consequences.

While most of us readily admit to faults in the areas of food and sex, we tend to see greed as a quality in other people rather than in ourselves. We see it in the mega-rich with their conspicuous spending, in city executives with their huge bonuses or in corrupt politicians taking bribes. We think that all greedy people are corrupt or rich, probably both, and since I'm neither corrupt nor rich, logically, I am not greedy. By thinking like this, we avoid facing our own greed. We fail to see that greed is not an all-or-nothing event; it is a thought that exists on a spectrum from weak to strong, but it affects us all. It is a subtle influence constantly present in all the decisions that everybody makes about material things. Our communal happiness and our individual happiness depend on our ability to acknowledge and curb our greed.

It comes as a surprise to most people when they discover that greed was a problem for the fathers and mothers of the desert. After all, these monks and nuns had purposely chosen to give up all material wealth and in the case of some of them, very considerable wealth. Yet those who were poor by choice still had to wrestle with thoughts about wanting more, just as those who become rich by choice are often driven by a demonic desire for still more wealth. Greed is a part of everybody's make up, whether we are rich or poor, whether we choose a simple life or whether we pursue a life of luxury.

During my thirty years working as a teacher, I was struck by the extraordinary growth in what were considered normal material possessions for a young teenager. Apart from expensive clothing like a suit, the most valuable possession of most teenagers thirty years ago was a watch. Now to the watch has been added the almost essential mobile phone, the 'everybody's got one' MP3 player and the increasingly common laptop. This of course does not apply to those excluded by poverty;

but while the number of people in Britain living in poverty has grown during the last thirty years, so has the wealth of the majority who are not poor. The reasons for this economic pattern would take us into political areas outside the scope of this book, but the channels through which the increased wealth has flowed are very relevant to the topic of greed. So let's begin by understanding how greed works generally and then we will be in a better position to see how it works in a consumer culture.

GREEDY MONKS

We all have a spontaneous understanding of how gluttony and lust work but we need guidance to understand greed. Greed begins with apparently harmless thoughts, Cassian tells us, and he explains how this works in the life of a monk. The monk begins to think that 'what is supplied in the monastery is inadequate and can hardly sustain a healthy and robust body'. The thought develops: 'the monk ponders how he can get hold of at least one penny'. When he has achieved that 'then he is distracted with the still more serious concern of what to buy with it and how he can double it'. Even thinking about how to double a penny can be a sign of greed and can unsettle us. This in turn leads to disillusionment with the way things are in the monastery and the monk cannot put up with things any longer. He complains that if he doesn't leave where he is currently living, 'he will perish on the spot'. And so he seeks excuses to leave the monastery.

The monk who stores up money and possessions, even in small amounts, moves to the edge of the community, becoming an observer, ready to find an excuse to leave. This then becomes a self-fulfilling prophecy because he complains that others are given more than he is and that he is treated like a stranger. He becomes more and more angry, demanding more and more, even what he never previously possessed. Cassian invokes the memory of biblical villains who have exemplifled this and in particular Judas Iscariot, who stole from the funds for the poor and betrayed Jesus for thirty pieces of silver.

The picture then is of a monk being drawn away from his true setting by the magnets of money and possessions. Yet it is also true that the magnetic attraction of things is something that can be switched off inside us; unlike the magnetic attraction of food and sex which are integral to our humanity, the attraction of money is not inevitable and it can be refused. To a greater extent than the other two, it is a thought that begins in the mind, thus it is the way that the monk builds up a story about his real needs not being met that is the prelude to seeking money. This story is the beginning of greed, not some natural impulse or urge that the monk fails to resist. The story we tell ourselves about ourselves is the origin of greed.

Similarly the outcome of greed is not some passing overindulgence in an urge: not a surfeit or drunkenness, the effects of which wear off, or illicit sexual activity which has an end-point. Rather, the outcome of greed is to leave the monastic life altogether, either to leave it psychologically by complaining the whole time from within, or to leave it physically by departing in search of something better.

It is no wonder then that St Benedict calls private ownership 'this evil practice' and insists that it must be 'uprooted and removed from the monastery' (RB, 33:1). Resisting the demon of money and possessions is very much a mental battle. The monk has to believe that what the monastery provides is adequate. So St Benedict follows his chapter on the evil of private ownership with a chapter on 'The Distribution of Goods According to Need' (RB, 34). This is the mirror image of private ownership, in which the abbot must make sure that everybody's legitimate needs are met. 'In this way all members will be at peace.' He continues, 'First and foremost, there must be no word or sign of grumbling, no manifestation of it for any reason at all' (RB,

34:5-6). Benedict is not saying a cheerful 'oh well we mustn't grumble'; he sees grumbling as the seedbed of vice, especially the vice of greed. So a balance is required in the monastery between the abbot ensuring that everybody has what they need and the tendency of monks to imagine that they need more.

What emerges from both these accounts is how deeply seriously greed was taken by the founders of the monastic tradition. The two basic insights that they offer can be readily applied to the lives of ordinary people today. Firstly, greed has its origins in the mental picture we have of our life and its needs. Secondly, if we get that mental picture wrong, it is a potential source of disintegration in the lives not only of individuals but also of communities. Armed with those monastic insights about how greed actually works, we can now look again at consumer culture.

CONSUMING HAPPINESS

Contemporary Western society probably has more material goods owned by more people than any other culture in history. We looked earlier at the break up of our food supply into a global sequence of treatment, packaging, transportation, marketing and selling that culminates in a purchase from a supermarket or fast-food outlet. Between the food grower and the person who eats it there is now a complex and long-distance relationship. The same can also be said now of most of the things we purchase. Everything has been consumerised. This is not in itself a bad thing and is partly responsible for a better quality of life in the developed world. The problem is the way that it usually plays out in our lives. When we have more we want more. In particular, the consumer culture tries to persuade us that more things mean more happiness: the marketing upon which the consumer culture is based is always about more, never about less.

Our Western culture is saturated with goods. The economically stable individuals and households who make up the majority of our population have more stuff than they actually need. While they might be persuaded to buy some more or different versions of what they already have, business recognises this material saturation and so the present thrust of consumerism is towards selling culture as well as things. Having saturated the world of our material needs, consumerism is now taking over our need for cultural goods such as music, entertainment and even moral purpose. The Disney Corporation is a classic example; this company sells stories in a hundred and one different formats: as films in cinemas, as DVDs, as books, as themed clothes, as theme parks, as a TV channel. These are material things but fundamentally people are buying stories, the stories that make up the Disney culture.

Disney stories carry all sorts of moral messages such as good triumphing over evil, but that is not the story that matters as regards activating my greed. The story that touches my greed is that Disney is educational and helpful, so we must go on buying Disney products in order to be a good and happy family. The message behind every movie and book, behind every theme park and T-shirt is that our children's world needs Disney. So they absolutely must go to see the next Disney movie, which we'll also want to give them on DVD as a birthday present. They will be happier if they live the full Disney experience; and thousands of families around the world buy into this deeper message as they flock to Disneyland. This is the new pilgrimage that children desire, a rite of passage into the meaning of life according to Disney. Where once morality and meaning were available as part of our free cultural inheritance, now corporations sell them to us as products.

It is not only the sellers of moral stories who sell culture; even the manufacturers of purely material products are joining in the quest to sell meaning. The way a product is marketed now tells us not only about the material pleasure it gives but also about its wider moral purpose. This orange juice is not only thirst-quenching and healthy, it also puts you back in touch with nature. These trainers will not only enable you to run faster, they will extend what you can achieve in life. Many brands now propose that they are about more than the material stuff. Brands marketed in this way claim to offer freedom of spirit but the reality that they seek to create is in fact an addiction to consumption.

Nike even has a section of its website called 'Addicts Gallery' where runners can post comments like this from Raul: 'I am at the will of a higher purpose.' On the video clip accompanying it, we see Raul go running in Nike kit and then hear him say: 'I have plugged into a higher purpose, left this world and come back changed. I am addicted.' Like Disney for children, so Nike for adults: they give people a 'higher purpose' through their brand. The companies may congratulate themselves that they are serving a higher purpose but this is basically the commercial exploitation of spirituality. A statement such as 'I am at the will of a higher purpose' that is used for marketing purposes has a corrosive effect on our understanding of personal identity and on our sense of the sacred. Even our souls are now consumerised, and marketing is destroying people's spiritual imagination. Unlike gluttony and lust, greed is a vice of the imagination and the mind before it is a vice of the body. So Disney, Nike and the other great corporations now inhabit our imagination, the place where greed is generated. Once planted there they can make us endlessly greedy. And that is exactly what they are doing.

RESISTING THE GREEDY CULTURE

So we live in a culture where shopping is virtuous and where greed is the hidden agenda. How can we overcome such overwhelming cultural forces and restore the purity of heart that we desire? We must first of all acknowledge that just as greed will always be present in our hearts in some form or other so consumer culture is going to be the place where we live even as we try to change that culture. We will need to shop at supermarkets and our children will need to buy trainers. Monks too will read the newspapers and use computers, travel by car and be tempted by the latest gadget. Yet this need not completely overwhelm our freedom of spirit and there are some simple ways that we can resist the consumer culture's takeover of our lives.

Once a year in Lent, we English Benedictine monks have the custom of writing out what we call 'a poverty bill'. We write down an inventory of everything we have for our personal use and hand it to the abbot. It's a very revealing exercise and enables us to ask: do I need all this? I have the following rule of thumb: if I haven't used an item in the last twelve months since the last poverty bill then I probably don't need it, so I give it away. I recommend this practice to everybody; it is a wonderful way to heighten self-awareness about material possessions, is quite liberating and you may be amazed to discover what you don't need.

Discovering what we don't need leads into thinking about those products with names like 'Indulgence' (the name of a luxury soap, a brand of chocolates and a tour operator) or with strap-lines like 'because you're worth it' for hair products. We can see that these messages are selfconsciously aware that the products they propose are not necessary and yet in the naming they subtly suggest that while they are not necessary, these products will make us happy. They actually imply that if we are unhappy, this is what we need to cheer us up. Indeed, many people think of self-indulgence as a way of counteracting unhappiness; but it is at best temporary and at worst makes the problem worse. Once we recognise this marketing manoeuvre, it is easier to see that these products are indeed not necessary, that happiness comes from elsewhere and that we can give them a miss.

Turning to children, we need to work hard

to ensure that they are not entirely at the mercy of commercial interests. We can begin to do this by offering our children non-commercial stories from our religious, ethnic and local traditions. We can encourage their own imagination and we can get them to tell their own stories. We can celebrate those stories in our homes in all sorts of ways, helping children to act out their imaginings. Creative play is the best way for children to resist the takeover of their imagination. Many features of British schooling militate against this. For example, an early start to formal learning blocks a child's imagination; even though this actually depresses formal test results later in life, parents still push for an early start to the three Rs. But perhaps the biggest challenge to young people and to older people alike is the way we celebrate Christmas. Here there is enormous potential for creative play and spiritual imagination and yet it is the time of year when commercial forces are at their most predatory.

HAPPY CHRISTMAS?

The phrase 'Happy Christmas' is so common that we don't often stop to ask what it means to put those two words together. For many people it means 'may your celebration of Christmas be pleasurable', but following the thread of happiness running through this book it means 'may your celebration of Christmas purify your heart'. The idea that Christmas is a time for purity of heart seems far removed from most people's reality. While I rejoice that Christmas is primarily a religious festival and wish that more people could share that religious joy, my concern here is not simply the loss of the religious significance of Christmas. My concern in the context of this chapter is about how Christmas has been made into a celebration of greed with a thin veneer of 'giving' laid over it. The commercial world has taken over the popular imagination at Christmas and tells us that there are only two essential parts of the festival, namely, Christmas gifts and Christmas feasting. Shopping is the key to both these activities and over the shopping frenzy is laid a sentimental shortcut to purity of heart: one day a year of peace and goodwill, then back to normal.

Yet Christmas can become part of our continuous search for deep happiness if we prepare with the intention of finding purity of heart there. One approach to combating Christmas greed is not to become sanctimonious, but to poke intelligent fun at it as exemplified by the Canadian initiative called 'Buy Nothing Christmas'. This group points out on their website that giving at Christmas need involve buying nothing at all but simply giving what we already have or what we can make with our own hands. They want to liberate people from the marketing pressures that are increasingly a burden at Christmas.

Another important bulwark against consumer Christmas is Advent. Advent is the traditional month of preparation before Christmas, a time of fasting and intense prayer, a time of eager expectation. It is above all a time to celebrate waiting as a normal part of human experience, when the Christian tradition invites us to wait for the birth of a child. In Advent we rejoice that we are waiting, that there is still time to prepare a way for the Lord and we celebrate the virtue of patience. By contrast, the consumer world tells us not to wait but to 'buy now'. Greed cannot wait, so to learn to wait is a simple antidote to greed. Christmas has ceased to be about the happiness of a pure heart because Advent as a period of restraint and of waiting has disappeared. Most people presume that Christmas begins when Christmas products appear in the shops in November. For example, a journalist who visited Worth Abbey a few days before Christmas was astonished to find no sign of Christmas decorations anywhere. She couldn't grasp that we were still celebrating Advent and that we wouldn't start Christmas until the night of Christmas Eve. A credit card company once ran a Christmas campaign with the slogan: Visa takes the

127

waiting out of wanting. By contrast, Advent puts the waiting back into wanting. Advent-with-Christmas has the potential to teach us how to enjoy the purity of heart that comes from waiting. Happy Christmas? Yes, provided we wait for it.

THE DEMONS OF THE BODY

In the three chapters about the demons of the body (gluttony, lust and greed) we have been seeking ways to place a filter between those thoughts that urge us to be self-indulgent and the actual carrying out of those thoughts.

We could call this an Advent discipline: wait before acting. Choose with self-awareness how to eat, how to express sexuality and how to use possessions. I have offered a critique of the consumer culture that tells us that the urges to self-indulgence are the way not only to pleasure but also to happiness. Those who oppose this consumer culture can easily be caricatured as puritans and killjoys. Remember Amma Syncletica's observation that spiritual apathy is 'full of mockery'.

The basic challenge that these three chapters pose is this: to have a real interior life, to have the possibility of a truly spiritual life, we must have a discipline of the body that is not simply bodily. These chapters have not proposed a regime of bodily exercise (necessary as that is for our health), but they have proposed a way of approaching three fundamental bodily instincts. The monastic tradition proposes that our bodily instincts are an integral part of a wider framework.

Body, heart and soul must all be in tune with each other. To arrive at this degree of awareness is a lifetime's work. That is why it's so much easier to 'buy' a story that says our bodily instincts only make sense when we purchase a product. The marketing tells us that the meaning of our urges comes from purchasing things to gratify the urges. The Christian monastic tradition opposes that view by showing how the urges are linked to the heart and to the soul. If they are not working together then freedom is lost and unhappiness is the result. For example, pride in the soul can cause sexual licence in the body, gluttony in the body can cause sadness in the heart and anger in the heart can cause illness in the body. If the body is in tune with heart and soul, then our eating opens up our hearts to other people, our sexuality is an expression of love and our possessions are gifts to share.

This attitude also shapes the monastic view of the arts. Painting and sculpture, music and drama, architecture and liturgy: all these involve arranging the physical world in ways that lead beyond the visible. This explains why abbey churches, like cathedrals, have always been places of artistic beauty, unashamedly using material and financial resources to create places that offer people access to the hidden dimensions of heart and soul. While numbers attending church services have dwindled, the numbers visiting great churches continues to rise.

The Christian story is that God is at work in the physical realities not just in hearts and souls. This is expressed most vividly in the Christian doctrine of the resurrection of the dead. The risen Christ is the first example of a body remade in a new way, and this is the destiny of all those who share his Spirit. We persevere in trying to align our bodies with our hearts and souls because in so doing we are aligning them with God's work. The last book of the Bible, and the most misunderstood, is the Book of Revelation, where the author presents an apocalyptic vision of this world transformed by Christ. 'Behold I make all things new', says the Lord. In the end, literally, God will make all *things* new.

FIFTH THOUGHT:
Anger

He gives me peace from the feud
Psalm 55:18

MENTAL HEALTH

In 2004 it was estimated that over a third of Americans received some kind of psychotherapy. (In this chapter, I will use psychotherapy to mean all those practices that involve working with a trained mental health professional: for example, counselling, psychoanalysis, psychiatry.) In addition, Americans spent $13.5 billion on antidepressant drugs that year. Figures such as these are sometimes quoted to show that people have become overly dependent on psychotherapeutic activity of all kinds. While that may be so, I think they can also be seen as evidence of a healthy concern about mental well-being. Given that psychotherapy and psychotherapeutic drug treatments are comparatively recent, attitudes to mental health have clearly undergone a revolution in modern times. So can the advice of the desert fathers and mothers still be relevant after this revolution?

While classic psychoanalysis might answer no, a more recent development in psychological understanding would suggest that the answer is definitely yes. A brief look at history will help to explain this. The origins of classic psychoanalysis lie in the pioneering work of Sigmund Freud and what was nicknamed at the time his 'talking cure'. But this was not just any kind of talking; it was talking aimed at uncovering the client's unconscious world, a world which Freud and his successors charted for the first time. This world is entered by the client talking about their childhood, their family history and most importantly their dreams; in this way, subconscious and potentially negative forces from the past or from the present can be recognised and with the help of the therapist, they can be let go or relived in a positive way.

My own decision to seek psychoanalysis came about when I was working as Headmaster and leading the school through a complex development process. At a critical stage of this development, I was badly let down by an individual and found myself doubly burdened: burdened firstly by having to devote immense amounts of time to compensate for their action and secondly burdened by my own feeling of outrage at the episode. With help from others, I came to recognise that I was very angry and that my anger was my responsibility, not the other person's. If my anger was truly mine, then I had to do something about it and not just blame the other person. So I started psychoanalysis with a gifted therapist and continued once a week for eighteen months. The process included my talking about my current feelings and my dreams, as well as painting with children's finger-paints. I built a very positive relationship with the therapist and found the hour a week with her to be very therapeutic; we didn't actually solve or resolve any issues or problems but fairly quickly, as my perception of myself, others and life started to shift, I came to realise that this was not the point. The anger that had provoked my starting therapy began to evaporate, but not by addressing it head on; this therapeutic hour was a time when there were no goals or tasks to achieve, I just had to own my life and actions as mine, exploring in depth how I lived and loved, worked and relaxed. By concentrating on my interior world, I was freed from the anger.

Looking back after the therapy ended, I came to see that my anger came from being a very goal-oriented person. I resented this other person's actions threatening the achievement of my goals for the school's development. The therapy had enabled me to find a space where goals and development were not on the agenda. This was not to say that it was just about being rather than doing; crucially, this therapeutic space enabled me to explore both my being and my doing as inextricably linked, but without reference to aims and ambitions. I learnt not only how to 'be myself', but also how to 'do myself', or act, in a different framework, more detached from the goal-oriented mind-set that fills the world of head teachers nowadays.

That experience taught me to value psychoanalysis, but it is a process far removed from the world of the desert fathers. Psychoanalysis does share with the desert tradition an emphasis on expressing thoughts to another person, but, as I discussed when looking at ways to master sexual thoughts, there the similarity ends. The therapist has a dialogue with the client, encourages the client to speak about childhood and dreams, and then uses their training to help the client see patterns and possibilities. The desert father, by contrast, simply listens and then offers a 'word to live by', meaning a word of scripture as a medicine to cure the thoughts that are troubling the monk. So while psychoanalysis, in the name of a particular school of thought, seeks to analyse the subconscious, the desert tradition, in the name of Christ, seeks to remove thoughts.

RATIONAL ALTERNATIVE

Alongside the development of the psychoanalysis that has its origins in Freud, there arose in the second half of the twentieth century another approach to psychotherapy. This approach is called Cognitive Behaviour Therapy, where the emphasis is on behaviour rather than the subconscious. The process sets out to change conscious behaviour rather than to explore the unconscious past. One of the earliest and now most widespread of these approaches is called Rational Emotive Behaviour Therapy, REBT, and it was first used by Albert Ellis in America during the mid-1950s. He came to believe that what a person thinks and what they feel are intimately connected, so he set about showing clients how their feelings and reactions are in large part generated by their thoughts. Ellis himself summarises his approach in a passage of his that is widely reproduced:

> REBT is based on the assumption that what we label our 'emotional' reactions are largely caused by our conscious and unconscious evaluations, interpretations, and philosophies. Thus, we feel anxious or depressed because we strongly convince ourselves that it is terrible when we fail at something or that we can't stand the pain of being rejected. We feel hostile because we vigorously believe that people who behave unfairly to us absolutely should not act the way they indubitably do, and that it is utterly insufferable when they frustrate us.

His insistence on the irrational origins of destructive feelings leads him to oppose some commonly held assumptions about emotions. No matter what kind of negative stimulus

137

impinges on a person, whether it is a personal failure or a physical attack, there is no need for a person to become angry.

REBT gives people full leeway to feel strong negative emotions, such as sorrow, regret, displeasure, annoyance, rebellion, and determination to change social conditions. It believes, however, that when they experience certain self-defeating and unhealthy emotions (such as panic, depression, worthlessness, or rage), they are usually adding an unrealistic and illogical hypothesis to their empirically-based view that their own acts or those of others are reprehensible.

So, although failing a history test at school may be 'reprehensible', there is no need for the student to add 'the unrealistic or illogical hypothesis' that failing a history test means that they are useless at history. They simply need to revise harder or differently.

Ellis devised a simple 'ABC' to explain this approach to clients. A for action is the event that starts off the chain of thoughts and feelings. B for belief is the thought that causes us to see the event in a certain way. C for consequence is the reaction of emotion and behaviour that follows in response to the original event seen in this way. Most people assume that A provokes C and that, consequently, they are powerless to stop C. REBT challenges that assumption and insists that the emotional response comes from the thought not from the event, that one's emotion and behaviour come from one's chosen belief system and not from the other person's action. The other person's action may stimulate our beliefs into reacting, but without those beliefs we would react quite differently.

Here is a simple example using REBT:

A) A friend passed me in the street without speaking to me

B)
  a. He's ignoring me because he doesn't like me
  b. For me to value myself, people must like me
  c. So he's telling me that I'm worthless as a person
C) Feeling: anger and depression
   Behaviour: avoid the former friend

With a different belief system at B the example now goes:

A) A friend passed me in the street without speaking to me
B)
  a. He probably has something on his mind

139

and didn't notice me
   b. He is a friend no matter what state of
      mind he's in
   c. I'd like to help him
C) Feeling: concern
   Behaviour: call round to see the friend

So our own belief system and not the other person's behaviour is the key factor in determining our emotional and behavioural reactions.

Our internal belief system has some rational beliefs and some irrational ones, where irrational means self-defeating. For example, the belief that we always need love and approval from those significant to us and that we must avoid their disapproval is irrational. Its irrationality lies in the fact that we literally defeat ourselves by handing our well-being over to a whole host of significant others. A more rational belief is that love and approval are good and we will seek them when we can, but they are not absolutely essential all the time from all significant others.

Another self-defeating belief is one which can be unwittingly fostered by a popular notion of psychotherapy. This is the belief that events in the past are the cause of our problems and that they influence our feelings and behaviours now. Again, this literally takes our present life out of our control and hands control to past events. A more rational approach is that our current beliefs cause our reactions, while we accept that we learnt those beliefs in the past. We can change what we learnt in the past and react differently now.

Such rational thinking majors on realism and will not accept our irrational tendency to catastrophise, i.e. to saythat someone is awful when they are simply annoying, to say that we can't stand something when we simply prefer something else, or to insist that someone (usually me) absolutely must do this when we mean that we would like to do it. REBT is not so much 'positive thinking', which seeks to be permanently optimistic, it is rather realistic thinking that keeps emotions, both positive and negative, within bounds.

This is not the same as the repression of emotions, far from it. It is rather choosing a belief system that will generate the right emotions that will lead to human fulfilment. It is about a way of living that makes discerning choices and believes in taking action to avoid that which is psychologically destructive. The anxiety-producing ideas *precede* the emotions, so if we review what we think then we can alter what we feel. Emotive behaviour can be rationally directed.

So, as I suggested earlier, while psychoanalysis is far removed from the desert tradition, REBT comes very close to it. Interestingly, Ellis quotes approvingly from the ancient Greek tradition of the Stoics, the

141

third-century BC philosophers who influenced the desert tradition very strongly. The great Stoic philosopher Zeno was as self-disciplined in his approach to life as the desert fathers, and as those who practise REBT. For Zeno, the passions were 'irrational and unnatural movements in the soul'. The Stoic view is that human desire and feeling should be consciously directed towards the virtues and that nothing should shake us in our determination to be virtuous. The passions, for the Stoic, are those appetites and fears over which we have lost control, which invade our minds with their 'irrational movement', similar to the 'irrational beliefs' of REBT. Both schools hold that we can choose what we believe to be of value and we can direct our emotions in that direction rather than allow ourselves to be overwhelmed with negative passion. This ancient philosophy has never really gone out of fashion, as is seen by the enduring popularity of *The Meditations of Marcus Aurelius*, the Stoic thoughts of a second-century Roman emperor.

Thus the 'thoughts' of the desert tradition share common ground with the Stoic view of the 'passions' and of the 'irrational beliefs' of REBT, in particular when it comes to the first of the 'thoughts of the heart': anger.

IS THERE ANY POINT IN
GETTING ANGRY?

The desert tradition insists that anger is a thought always to be avoided, a demon to whom we should never give in. Cassian calls it a 'deadly poison . . . that must be totally uprooted'. He quotes scripture at length to show the harm that can come to one who is angry, destroying right judgement, wisdom and the interior light of contemplation. He insists that 'man's anger does not work God's righteousness', and then goes on to challenge those who seek to justify anger directed towards those who do wrong. He is disdainful of those who quote passages of scripture that say 'God was angry with Israel', saying that such passages are figurative and notes stingingly that if people take that metaphor literally how will they cope with other passages that suggest God was 'asleep like a man drunk with wine'. To use scripture as a source for justifying anger, he says, is to derive death from the very place where the medicine of salvation is found.

Cassian is particularly critical of a monk who gets angry with the wrongdoing of another brother, which he sees as an example of taking the speck of wrongdoing out of the other person's eye before removing the plank of wrath in our own. What Cassian calls 'the function for anger placed quite appropriately within us' is only beneficial for one purpose: when we become angry with our own faults and failings. He cites approvingly St Paul's injunction that we must not let the sun go down on our anger, emphasising the verse that follows, 'or else you will give the devil a foothold'. His conviction that anger against others should not be given the slightest hold over us is so intense that he even worries about whether 'do not let the sun go down on your anger' could be read as allowing anger for a short time. So he interprets this phrase as meaning firstly that our anger must be directed against our own faults, including our raging at others, and secondly that Christ is the sun. So before the darkness of our evil thoughts eclipses Christ in our hearts, we must direct our anger against those thoughts and drive them away.

He then goes on to reveal a remarkably wide knowledge of how those who claim that they are not angry can manifest the deepest anger by their actions. 'They maintain a rancorous spirit against those with whom they are upset . . . They neither approach them with an appropriate word nor speak to them with ordinary civility, and in this regard they do not consider themselves in the wrong because they do not demand vengeance for their annoyance.' Rather than bring it out into the open, 'they turn the poison of their wrath back to their own destruction, brooding over it in their hearts and in glum silence digesting it within themselves'. Simply controlling the symptoms does not root it out from the heart, and the darkness of rage can still blind us even when it is not made manifest; worse still, the radiance of God's Spirit is excluded from our hearts by the presence of the demon of rage.

Not content with removing anger from our own hearts, Cassian goes on to ask that we try to remove anger from the hearts of those who are angry with us, even if we think that we have done nothing to justify their anger. He notes the saying of Jesus that 'If you are offering your gift at the altar and there remember that your brother has something against you, leave your gift there at the altar, go first and be reconciled with your brother, and then come and offer your gift' (Matthew 5:23-4). It is easy to misread this passage, to assume it says 'you have something against your brother', but a careful reading shows that it applies to the brother being angry with you. Cassian takes 'offering your gift at the altar' to mean prayer offered to God, and he reminds monks that their principal task is to 'pray without ceasing' (1 Thessalonians 5:17), a quotation from St Paul that he cites frequently and to which he now adds another 'In every place lift up pure hands in prayer without anger or dissension' (1 Timothy 2:8). He points out that if we dare to pray when a

145

brother is angry, ignoring all these scriptural injunctions, we are offering only 'stubborn and rebellious hearts' to God. If we want to have a pure heart in prayer, we must seek out any aggrieved brother who, rightly or wrongly, has something against us. The Lord wants all to be saved and so we cannot pray if somebody is experiencing anger because of us. We have a responsibility to help that person lose their anger so that they too can once again find tranquillity and pray with a pure heart.

Cassian then explains why he is so rigid in his total prohibition of anger and in this he overlaps with REBT. He offers a very rational explanation; he wants each of us to be wholly responsible for our own virtue and to approach life in such a way that we do not depend upon the perfection of other people for our own well-being. In a passage that might have been written by Albert Ellis he writes:

The sum total of our improvement and tranquillity, then, must not be made to depend on someone else's willing, which will never be subject to our sway; it comes, rather, under our own power. And so our not getting angry must derive not from someone else's perfection but from our own virtue, which is achieved not by another person's patience but by our own forbearance.

Cassian turns finally to examine how some people choose to walk away from other people as a way of handling anger. So he looks at people who live as hermits—and those who live as monks—and notices that they can still find anger in their hearts even though there is nobody against whom to direct it. Instead they direct it against objects. He lists the meagre objects that a monk possesses and then enumerates the imperfections that can provoke anger: the pen is thick, the penknife is blunt, and the flint no longer sparks.

The monk must root out even this anger if he is to find purity of heart, the ultimate goal of the monastic life and the only way to true peace of mind.

Cassian concludes his teaching on anger with an extraordinary discussion about manuscripts, which again shows him cutting off all possible roots to justifying anger. In the Sermon on the Mount, just before the section quoted above about 'offering your gift at the altar', there is the verse 'whoever is angry with his brother shall be liable to judgement' (Matthew 5:22). Cassian informs us that some gospel manuscripts circulating among the desert fathers and mothers have the phrase 'without cause' added in and read 'whoever is angry with his brother without cause'. He insists that 'without cause' is an addition to the text made by people who think that it is sometimes acceptable to be angry. He says the

147

phrase is superfluous since no one, however irrationally upset, would say that he had no cause for anger. 'For patience does not achieve its goal in righteous anger but in not getting angry at all.'

A later generation of Christian authors will allow 'rational anger', by which they mean zeal for justice, a passionate rejection of evil rather than a response to personal slight. Yet all the monastic writers, those involved in community living, retain their outright condemnation of anger. As a monk, I find it better to be clearly against anger of all kinds and to support zeal for justice as something quite distinct. Nelson Mandela is a good example of somebody who combined zeal for justice with a lack of personal anger. He was zealous in bringing apartheid to an end in South Africa but still has friendly relations with his white former gaoler. Getting angry about a problem rarely improves the situation; what is needed is a zealous determination to overcome it.

CONCLUSION

Anger is a major issue in everybody's life and in the life of nations. How we handle it is a vital factor in determining our well-being and our happiness. The popular notions that it is good to 'let off steam' or that it is right 'to give those people a piece of my mind' are based on a very mechanistic view of human beings. We are not steam engines, we are rational beings who can make our own choices; we are not objects that can cut off a piece of our mind, we are whole people with integrated emotions. The insistence of the desert tradition that we must not give way to anger may seem at odds with the contemporary assumptions encapsulated in those popular sayings. Yet in REBT we see a school of modern thought that refuses to allow the takeover of our inner world by irrational outbursts of feeling.

The desert fathers and mothers can be seen as part of a wider spiritual tradition: the classic view that to be self-possessed is both possible and desirable. This ancient view goes back to the Stoics, as already noted, and finds its strongest early Christian expression among the first monks and nuns. In this tradition, the soul is rational and the expression 'the rational soul' is used to describe a person's inner world. The intrusion of disturbing thoughts is a demonic intrusion which upsets the rational equilibrium of the soul. Hence the thoughts and their demons can be analysed and systematically repelled by the rational soul. This classic tradition now finds a modern expression in cognitive behaviour therapies such as REBT. By contrast, Freud's insight was that the disturbing thoughts come not from demons, but from an irrational part of us that he labelled the unconscious. And the insight of modern psychiatry is that they come from chemical changes in the brain.

Demons, the unconscious, chemicals. Well, which is it? What is the source of our disturbing thoughts? There is no simple answer to that question and it continues to be disputed among scientific experts. My own experience as I have related it here teaches me that there is a time for one approach and a time for a different approach. I have benefited from both psychotherapy and from the classic workings of the rational soul. In this chapter I have offered an affirmation that the classic view of soul-making is still valid, that it has not simply been replaced by modern insights and can be one of the steps along the path to finding happiness. It sits alongside psychoanalysis and psychiatry as one way of addressing those emotions that disturb us, a way that will not be the right answer for everybody always, but one that many people apply day to day without the help of therapists or doctors.

SIXTH THOUGHT:
Sadness

My hope will never fade
Psalm 71:14

ARE MONKS SAD?

This book began by asking are monks happy and I answered by saying that monks are not unhappy, on the grounds that 'unhappy' has a much more focused sense than the ambivalent 'happy'. While monks are not unhappy, meaning that they are not miserable, nevertheless, they do experience sadness.

If somebody is experiencing real sadness, we can approach the situation from three different angles. A doctor could diagnose a physical illness. A psychiatrist might diagnose depression. A spiritual guide might discern one of the Eight Thoughts. The diagnosis by the doctor and the psychiatrist are outside the scope of this book. Our spiritual guide, Cassian, was well aware of the possibilities of truly devastating depression and recognised that even monks are occasionally overwhelmed by 'deadly despair' to such an extent that they take their own lives. The insights offered here from the monastic tradition can support those who experience sadness of all kinds, but they are no substitute for the medical treatment of depression. Those who experience 'deadly despair' need professional help as well as spiritual support.

This chapter deals with the more widespread phenomenon of sadness that includes experiencing 'the blues', thinking 'life's not fair' and saying 'I'm feeling rubbish'. One trend that we will not include is the meaning of the word 'sad' as currently used by young people. In that culture, situations and people are 'sad' if they are boring or old-fashioned, so 'sad' has become the ultimate youth insult. Teenagers might hurl 'you're so sad' at their parents as they storm from the room after being told they can't go to the party. In a world where everybody must be seen to be happily enjoying themselves, 'sad' has come to mean the absence of happiness as pleasure. In this context, when somebody is 'sad' they are not considered to be grieving or suffering from depression, they are seen to be lacking in opportunities to enjoy themselves and 'they ought to get out more'. That meaning of 'sad' is built on the identification of happiness with pleasure, and this whole book directly challenges such identification. By contrast with that meaning of sadness as the exterior lack of pleasure, this chapter is about sadness as the interior experience of darkness. Such sadness is not a lack of anything; it is a feeling in its own right.

From a physiological perspective, mood-swings are explained as alterations in the body's chemistry. As a regular jogger, I know that a good run lifts my mood, even in bad weather, because the exercise causes my body to produce serotonin, a chemical that has a 'feel good' effect. At the other end of the happiness spectrum, as a former teacher, I know that sitting in an airless room for a long period causes a downturn in class mood, with yawns and glum looks all round; at first I thought the cause was my lacklustre teaching, but as a five-minute break in the open air transformed the mood, I soon learnt that a lack of oxygen causes pupil gloom as much as poor teaching. In the case of jogging or classroom behaviour we can clearly see the physical origin of mood-swings. At one level, sadness is simply a severe downturn in mood caused by a chemical change. When the causes of the physical downturn in mood are themselves physical then we can deal with sadness relatively easily: take some exercise or open a window. When the causes are psychological then the situation is much harder to manage and it is these psychological causes that we will consider.

WHAT CAUSES SADNESS?

The causes of sadness and depression are not always clear, and sometimes 'the blues' or severe depression come upon us for no apparent reason. In his remarkable account of his own chronic depression entitled 'Darkness Visible', the American novelist William Styron offers the opinion that the root cause of depression is an unresolved loss. In his case, the death of his mother when he was aged 13, which involved an 'incomplete mourning', probably sowed the seed of his later depression.

Loss seems to be the principal trigger for the onset of many kinds of sadness and Cassian lists various losses that have this effect. Firstly, losing your temper; we nowadays forget that anger involves losing something, namely our balanced state of mind, so that sadness follows 'losing' our equilibrium. Anger as a major cause of sadness was already acknowledged by the desert fathers even before modern psychology identified unacknowledged anger as a source of depression. Then there is loss of money, loss of acquiring things that the mind was set on, loss of self-respect when some injury has been inflicted upon us. These losses are not the loss of a loved one; they are not the emotion of grief in death. The cliche 'nobody died' contains the important insight that if we are sad at the loss of some *thing* then we have the possibility of facing and overcoming the loss in ways that are so much harder when dealing with death.

Seeing sadness as a response to the loss of something can be the first step to overcoming it. But as with anger so with sadness, Cassian is adamant that events themselves do not cause depression. Sadness is not aroused in us by other people's faults, says Cassian. 'Rather, we are to blame.' Once again, the desert tradition and cognitive behaviour therapy coincide in asking us to take responsibility for our own feelings. The monastic tradition offers a very specific remedy.

HOPE

Hope is the surest remedy against sadness and so we have to take conscious steps to sustain hope. While we recognise the need to foster a loving attitude in children, nowadays people tend not to foster hope with the same self-conscious energy. Cassian invites us to exercise a discipline of hope. This means not placing our hope where it is subject to change and decay, avoiding reliance for our interior wellbeing on wealth and position. We are heading back to the primitive definition of happiness as luck if we have placed our hope in financial markets or promotion. The disappointments and the successes of our daily lives should both be treated with balance and not be the source alternately of sadness and elation. Hope is bigger than these, on a par with love, so that just as I do not determine my love for somebody just by my mood today so my hope should not be subject to passing events.

It's worth taking a moment to do an audit of

hope in our lives. What gets us out of bed in the morning? What do we most dread losing? What absorbs our spare time? The responses to these questions are the answer to the question: in what do I place my hope? To see how our hopes may need to change, consider the following questions. Apart from deferred household chores, what aspects of my life do I neglect? How much time and energy do I give to spiritual exercises? After work, how much energy do I have to build up love and relationships?

Sustaining hope is one of the surest ways of keeping sadness at bay and is an important aspect of both mental and spiritual health. As part of that, Cassian invites us to meditate on the promises of God about death and resurrection. Christians have in the last fifty years concentrated on building the kingdom of God on earth, but to follow Christ's teaching and example involves 'both now and forever', as the Christian tradition of prayer so clearly expresses it. People find it hard in our culture to express their thoughts and feelings about death as the ultimate challenge to hope. And even Christians these days are confused about the meaning of that hope-filled phrase in the creed: 'we look for the resurrection of the dead and the life of the world to come.'

LIFE'S NOT FAIR

Let's now look at some of the situations that cause sadness and see how we can bring hope to bear on them. Take the example of losing a job. I have known people who have been dismissed for lack of competence and been paid off so that they had no redress in law against what they saw as an unfair action. In some cases the employer may have acted unjustly, so it is not surprising when the person who has been fired becomes angry and depressed. Difficult as it is, though, the person still has to take responsibility for their personal response to the situation.

I have noticed the following patterns in people's responses. They are angry with the boss who sacked them: he never did like me, they say, and he had no right to fire me. They then rehearse in their mind how unfairly they have been treated, how unfair life is and how they'll probably never get another decent job. They say things like 'This is so unfair, I've done nothing wrong. I'm furious' and then the anger turns into resentment, 'I worked hard for that company and look how ungrateful they are.' Finally depression sets in: 'It's awful, I can't stand the humiliation, and my life is ruined.' At the extreme, people even contemplate suicide in such situations, feeling that life is now unbearable.

Yet it is not the loss of the job as such that has provoked this emotional and mental state. Rather a set of beliefs about life has been brought into play in response to the loss of the job. It is the hidden beliefs going round inside the person's head that cause the depression. These beliefs are along the lines: I do my job pretty well and my judgement of my performance is always right. My life should not be disrupted and a major disruption is bad for me. I definitely should not be treated this way and if I am then life is intolerably unfair. Life must not be like this. These beliefs lead people to 'catastrophise' the situation; namely, they turn a problem into a crisis. A calm look at such beliefs, however, reveals that they are unhelpful because they are unrealistic. So I will now outline a more realistic understanding of such a situation, with the caveat that this understanding is not something to present baldly to the depressed person. Rather, what follows is a framework that we can help such a person come to discover in time when they are ready to move on.

Firstly, the boss's assessment of competence is as valid as mine and he clearly disagreed with my own assessment. If they paid me off they clearly thought they would be better off without me. Secondly, disruptions to plans are part of life, they are not exceptional and I had no absolute right to assume that life would accord with my personal plans. Finally, every day thousands of people lose their jobs but rare indeed is the person who thinks that they were dealt with fairly when being told to go. This is a common experience; life is, precisely, like this.

A more realistic and helpful set of beliefs would be something like the following. When I look back at the good work that I did and the friends that I made, I realise that these are happy memories of good times so I'm disappointed to be leaving. My life is going to be disrupted now, so it will be financially tougher and I would much prefer that this hadn't happened. But I can start looking for another job, maybe even another career and that might lead on to unexpected good things. In summary, the rational beliefs acknowledge that there is a serious problem and the irrational beliefs insist that there is an unbearable crisis. And it is the thought that we are experiencing an unbearable crisis that causes sadness and even depression.

This is a tough analysis, some may think an unsympathetic one. Those experiencing such emotions about losing a job or losing something else need sensitive support not telling off. Simply saying 'pull yourself together and behave rationally' is not the whole answer. We need to help people find the space where they can face these difficult truths about their situation.

The first time I can recall experiencing 'the

blues' as an adult, I didn't even realise what was happening to me. It was a very minor and short-lived experience but the shape of it is instructive. I'd been at an important meeting that morning where what seemed to me to be some very poor decisions were made and the points that I made had been ignored. After lunch, I found I couldn't function properly and I had no energy to try. So I talked to another monk and he helped me to see that I was experiencing the demon of sadness. I am an innately upbeat person and so sadness didn't really feature in my repertoire as far as I was concerned. But I had to admit that I was now sad. At this distance, I can still remember the feeling, but I can't remember the content of the discussions and decisions that caused it. The emotion is still strong, but the thought is weak. It was a discussion that had caused the gloom to descend on me, a series of thoughts, some expressed and some unexpressed, so it was thoughts that had triggered the feeling. My arguments had been ignored. My belief was that my point of view is always correct and that it is unbearable when I do not win the argument. That is a pretty common but irrational belief. Cassian describes among the causes of sadness 'that which proceeds from an irrational turn of mind'. When loss meets an irrational frame of mind then sadness and depression are liable to follow. The way out is to notice that we have placed our hope in unhelpful beliefs ('I am always right' or 'I will never lose an argument') and, having noticed them, choose to leave them aside. Then we can place our hope in beliefs worthy of our trust and regain our perspective.

LOSS OF PERSPECTIVE

One of the most disturbing things that we can lose in life is perspective. To lose perspective is to experience everything as negative and not to know how to get out of it. This is a very serious loss of hope, although it is still short of the 'deadly despair' discussed earlier. A real difficulty here is that a loss of perspective is almost impossible to perceive in ourselves and it needs somebody else to lead us gently to regain our perspective. Once regained, we might look back and see what we had lost; but at the time, there was no way we could see that we had lost it.

Following the transmission of the TV series The Monastery, a lot of people contacted us to share their problems and ask for our help. In general, these were written communications, so we offered whatever comfort is possible in writing and suggested that they contact a local priest or professional for further help. We could not offer to see them all personally as the number ran into thousands. As an exception, a friend asked me if I would personally see one particular person, a psychiatrist.

A married man with grown-up children, he had clearly had a successful career, but as he approached retirement he felt overwhelmed by emotions that he did not understand. Watching the TV series, he said, had brought him a glimmer of hope and that was why he wanted to speak to me. As we spoke, his depression was palpable but there was more to it than that. He said that he didn't want to see a psychiatrist because he thought he knew exactly what they would do and say, and he didn't want that. So what did he need? He had no idea and that was his problem. He agreed to see his GP for anti-depressant medication to provide a window through which we could explore matters further. He did not entertain thoughts of suicide but life held no joy; there was no crisis in his family relationships but family life seemed empty and he went to church only occasionally. His life seemed to be pointless and the future seemed equally bleak. Yet coming to Worth to sit in the abbey church and talking to me brought him great solace. We came to realise that beyond the depression there lay the wider issue of hope: he lacked the virtue of hope and the only place where he found it again was in the physical setting of our church. This was not so much finding religion but rather finding a visceral experience of hope; hope had ceased to be an abstraction and was now a core need that was only met in a monastic context.

He came on two retreats at Worth and found them profoundly affecting. From hope started to flow a renewed sense of love, love of family and love of life itself. Gradually, very gradually, a renewed sense of life began to flow and with it came an engagement with church as personal not formal. He has regained a sense of perspective. Hope has proved to be the existential foundation of faith and love.

REMORSE

Cassian adds two insights about sadness that are surprising to modern readers. He explains why sadness can be a source of joy and why sadness makes us unhappy; the first seems contradictory and the latter a statement of the obvious, but remember, the monastic tradition has a very particular view of happiness.

Cassian recommends one kind of sadness as good for us, namely, sadness at our own faults. So there is a good and a bad sadness, and the good sadness is grief at my own wrongdoing. 'With a kind of joy, and quickened by the hope of its own progress, the sadness at my sins retains all its gracious courtesy and forbearance.' Recognising my own faults, while truly a sadness, can be a source of joy since it leads me to change for the better and helps me to be patient with other people.

Contrast this with sadness directed at others which is 'very harsh, impatient, rough, full of rancour and barren grief and punishing despair . . . since it is irrational'. Allowing myself to get upset at other people's faults has three bad effects. Firstly, I become impatient with other people and can become overwhelmed with despair at their faults. Then this leads me away from the one sadness that might rationally help me, namely, sadness at my own faults. Finally, it affects my prayer and while it does not destroy the monk's ability to pray, it nevertheless 'removes the efficacy of prayer'. In other words, the effect of prayer should be to foster in the one praying the fruits of the Spirit such as love, joy and patience, but sadness directed towards others' faults destroys these qualities. Cassian implies that somebody at prayer who is gripped by negative sadness is wasting their time until they have stepped away from their anger and depression. This sounds harsh but in fact this is provable in practice: no matter how much I pray, if I am continually getting upset with other people I will not be growing in joy and peace, which are the fruits of true prayer. So Cassian's particularly creative insight about depression is his distinction between the sadness at self, which is a source of joy, and the sadness at others, which is an obstacle to spiritual living.

CATHOLIC GUILT?

If the only kind of sadness that Cassian encourages is sadness about our own sins, you may be wondering if this isn't just good old-fashioned Catholic guilt. To answer that we need to distinguish 'feeling guilty' from 'being guilty'. When people experience guilt, they are recognising that they have done wrong and this insight can lead in either a destructive or a constructive direction. Some people simply feel guilty and stop there, just wallowing in guilt so to speak. They may respond in this way in order to make the guilty feeling a compensation for their wrongdoing: saying 'see how bad I feel about this' lets them off the hook of doing something about it. In this case, guilt blocks positive action. Another kind of guilt that blocks action is the guilt that is accompanied by fear of discovery and punishment: 'what if I am found out' somebody may say to themselves, and fear of punishment then blocks any progress because to make amends may first need an admission of guilt. We might characterise these two as 'wallowing guilt' and 'fearful guilt': these are what are known popularly as 'Catholic guilt' and they are destructive because they paralyse a person who has done wrong and leaves them no way forward.

By contrast, the true Catholic tradition promotes a positive response to justifiable guilt. It's worth emphasising that justifiable guilt means guilt in response to real wrongdoing, not in response to feeling awkward or infringing a rule; so feeling awkward about your child's behaviour in public or about accidentally getting a free ride on the bus create embarrassment not guilt. The Catholic tradition sees justifiable guilt about a serious matter as a positive asset and a prelude to growth. We need to feel remorseful about today's failure to love in order to love more tomorrow. To have no sense of guilt after serious wrongdoing disables our ability to grow as people; at an extreme, lack of remorse is a sign of a pathological state of mind, a severe personality disorder, as seen when we call somebody a pathological killer if they kill with no sense of guilt. The ability to feel justifiable guilt is an important part of normality; properly understood, sadness is a vital component of conscience. And having a well-formed, active conscience is an important aspect of purity of heart.

A positive response to guilt is what the Catholic tradition calls repentance and it lies at the heart of how the desert fathers respond when they find themselves overcome by negative thoughts. The joy that comes from sadness at personal sin is achieved by being completely honest with ourselves as quickly as possible, as illustrated by an Abba Poemen story. A brother said to Poemen, 'If I fall into a shameful sin, my conscience devours and accuses me saying: "Why have you fallen?" The old man said to him: "At the moment when he goes astray if he says, I have sinned, immediately the sin ceases."' The whole emphasis is neither on the past nor even on the present, but on healthy living in the future. Poemen again: a brother came to Abba Poemen saying: 'What does it mean to repent of a fault?' The old man said: 'Not to commit it again in the future.' Having experienced sadness at our sins, we will be motivated to make amends and to avoid wrongdoing in the future. This is purity of heart, true interior happiness, where a sense of guilt does not burden us but sets us free for the future.

THE PSALMS

One of the great remedies for all the thoughts is praying the psalms, and they are especially helpful in coping with sadness. The psalms remind us that we are not alone in our struggles with the demons. The psalm writers share the depths and the heights of their human experience, as they pour their hearts out before God. All the demons are here and so the psalms remind us not only that God is with us, but also that we have companions along the way. These companions can inspire us and encourage us because they made their struggles into prayer. Their prayers offered up to heaven are some of the most down-to-earth ever written, full of cursing and anger as well as joy and delight. Modern sensibilities are such that most churches today omit the so-called cursing psalms, which robs them of the fullness of their human experience. As we strive to achieve purity of heart, the psalms show us how even our failures are part of the process.

One psalm is particularly apt for the demon of sadness. Psalm 88 begins 'Lord my God, when I cry out to you in the night' and the middle section reads: 'You have plunged me to the bottom of the grave, in the darkness, in the depths.' Normally, a psalm full of so much sadness would end with an upbeat affirmation of faith in God. For example, the verse spoken by Jesus on the cross, 'My God, my God, why have you forsaken me' is a quotation from Psalm 22 that goes on to say 'I shall proclaim your name, Lord . . . praise you to the full assembly.' But Psalm 88 has no such ending; it is total despair from start to finish. It concludes: 'You have deprived me of friends and companions, and all that I know is the dark.'

When people in deep grief or despair tell me that they cannot pray, I encourage them simply to read this psalm. Through it they can express to God the full extent of their sadness with no artificial striving after consolation. Simply knowing that this experience can be offered to God can be the beginnings not so much of consolation as of moving on to life beyond sadness. Perhaps the one redeeming feature of sadness is that it does pass, so that, with support, it can be survived.

SEVENTH THOUGHT:
Vanity

Why love what is vain and chase after illusions?
Psalm 4:1

The previous six thoughts all operate either in a person's body (gluttony, lust and greed) or in the heart and mind (anger, sadness and spiritual apathy.) These are all-too-human failings and we can recognise them clearly in ourselves and in others. The final pair of the Eight Thoughts, however, is active in the spiritual dimension itself. These are the demons of the soul, vanity and pride, hidden from view and hard to detect.

The Latin for vanity is *vanagloria* from *vanus* meaning empty and *gloria* here denoting reputation, so *vanagloria* has the literal meaning 'empty reputation'. Vanity is the admiration of one's own achievements and skills as well as of one's looks and qualities. Cassian considers vanity to be the most subtle of all the demons because 'where virtue abounds vanity is always a danger'. In other words, when we have mastered a virtuous skill, especially the spiritual skill of containing the demons of the body and the mind, just when we think we've got the spiritual life cracked, this is when vanity strikes.

Vanity becomes evident through attitudes such as complacency about our skills and qualities, sometimes combined with narcissism and self-admiration. It differs from pride because pride does not necessarily involve the desire for praise. Pride involves placing

175

ourselves above others and ultimately placing ourselves above God, usurping a rank that is not ours. We will look at pride more fully in the next chapter.

It's worth asking how these subtle demons of the soul relate to the modern and unsubtle phenomenon called celebrity. Is celebrity simply the latest expression of vanity and pride. A celebrity is often described as somebody who is famous for being famous.Whereas in previous eras people were famous for their achievements, now people become famous by simply appearing in the mass media. This phenomenon is not as new as we think. 'Notoriety, or the making of a noise in the world, has come to be considered a great good in itself, and a ground of veneration.' This very contemporary observation was made in 1849 by Cardinal John Henry Newman. He could have had *Hello* magazine in mind when he wrote: 'Notoriety, or, as it may be called, newspaper fame, becomes a sort of idol, worshipped for its own sake.' The arrival of the modern newspaper in Victorian Britain meant that 'never could notoriety exist as it does now, in any former age of the world.' So notoriety and celebrity are long-established parts of modern culture made possible by the mass media.

While some celebrities are high achievers in sport or in entertainment, for example, some are just people who did nothing more than appear in *Big Brother.* Yet celebrity is not something that happens inside a person, it is not something that people choose for themselves; celebrity is conferred on somebody by the public and by journalists. It is therefore different from vanity, which is an attitude held by the vain person and by nobody else; each of us is responsible for our own vanity. Nevertheless, celebrity facilitates vanity and modest celebrities are not the norm.

This celebrity that encourages vanity enters deeply into the culture of young people. It is not uncommon nowadays for the age-old enquiry 'what do you want to be when you grow up?' to be met with the reply 'famous'. When a friend received this reply from a pre-teenage girl, he asked her 'famous for what?' and she replied 'just famous'. In other words, this is fame without substance; there is nothing to it. This takes us back to the literal meaning of the Latin *vanagloria*; for this young girl, celebrity has become the same as 'empty reputation'.

EMPTINESS

So the cult of celebrity seems to be eating into people's souls and making vanity something to be desired rather than avoided. We've already noticed that pursuing demons rather than rejecting them is often seen as the modern path to happiness. The desire for 'empty reputation' is a good point at which to consider why this should be so. The answer may be that many people today experience life as empty of meaning and so cast around to avoid facing their personal emptiness. In our society, there is a much reduced sense of belonging to a community or even to a family; with the decline of religion and the collapse of twentieth-century philosophies such as communism, people do not have a vision or a philosophy beyond 'feeling good' and not harming others, though even the latter is under threat in some areas. So people are minimally connected to each other and have limited visions of what their lives are about. The need to keep feeling good becomes the insatiable driving force of this empty experience of life. The rich can, of course, buy more 'feel good' products than the poor, but the experience is still felt by all social classes. So people turn to the demons as the best source of feeling good. Paradoxically, then, the flight from 'emptiness' may be what is motivating people to embrace not only 'empty reputation', but all the other 'empty' demons as well.

I recently overheard a conversation between a man and a woman in their twenties. He had clearly not made some previously agreed arrangement for Saturday. 'So we've got nothing for this Saturday night', she screamed.

She swore at her boyfriend and looked distraught, muttering 'What are we going to do?' He made some phone calls and then triumphantly announced that he'd fixed something. At which point the girl was transformed and embraced him warmly. An unconscious fear of meeting our emptiness may well drive people to seek out the excitement that the demons offer.

Each of the Eight Thoughts seems to offer something to fill the void. The three demons of the body, gluttony, lust and greed, are obvious examples of this. In their own way, the three thoughts of the heart can also fill the emptiness. An underlying state of anger is an effective way of keeping the void at bay; I'm so busy telling everybody off that I don't look at myself. In a different way, depression is an emotion that comes unbidden to fill the space created by many different kinds of loss, loss being a sense of emptiness where there once was fullness. Finally, spiritual apathy is a refusal to be spiritually still and face the inner emptiness. So too with vanity that fills my life with bogus self-admiration in order to stave off the sight of my own emptiness.

So as people run away from the void in their lives by embracing the demons, they find that the demons themselves are empty. This reminds me of a picture painted by the celebrated American artist Edward Hopper. His painting entitled 'Excursion into

179

Philosophy' shows a middle-aged man sitting gloomily on the edge of a bed reading a book; behind him on the bed is a half-naked woman. The painting's ironic subtitle is 'On re-reading Plato too late'.

During the course of this book, I have referred several times in passing to Jesus's Sermon on the Mount and in particular to the Beatitudes. It's now time to look at them in more depth as they constitute a profound and unexpected solution to life's perceived emptiness and vanity.

THE BEATITUDES

A beatitude is a biblical saying that begins 'Blessed are . . .' and it presents translators with a challenge because the ancient Greek word *makarios* is difficult to render in any modern language. Somebody who is *makarios* is to be congratulated because God is especially close to them; that is the correct meaning of blessed. But the word blessed is disliked by modern translators because secular people don't understand divine blessing. The use of the patronising phrase 'bless him' and its shortened form 'bless' demonstrate this, with their implication that blessing is a sympathetic consolation prize for losers. This is the exact opposite of the biblical meaning,

180

where blessing is God's first prize for his winners. So modern translators have gone for 'happy are . . .' Some readers of modern bibles might therefore be wondering why I have not concentrated on those biblical phrases beginning 'happy are . . .' since they would appear to contain the complete answer to a Christian view of happiness. But 'happy' is a misleading translation of *makarios*, a fact seen clearly when we get to '*makarioi*, those who mourn'; whatever else you may say about grieving people, the one thing they are not is happy. One very recent translation of the Beatitudes begins each phrase with 'congratulations to . . .' and this is closer to the mark. So what are the Beatitudes really saying

The first three Beatitudes are:
Blessed are the poor in spirit, for theirs is the kingdom of God.
Blessed are those who mourn, for they shall be comforted.
Blessed are the meek, for they shall inherit the earth.

Poverty of spirit, meekness, grief, these are qualities of people without vanity. Visibly, they appear to have lost something: wealth or assertiveness or a loved one, but out of this absence God draws another invisible reality, the kingdom of God. The kingdom is not a place but the power of God at work in life, and this power works best when people admit that there is something missing. The vain cannot know this power because they are operating under their own steam and fill life with their own stuff, so the power of the other cannot find a way in.

The truth that we find hard to accept about life is that to be human is to be vulnerable. We would rather believe that to be human is to be secure. So we spend our energy on looking secure and convincing ourselves that we are secure. That is vanity. We should instead work at accepting our vulnerability as a gift, a gift that enables us to receive other people's love and help. In turn, other people's vulnerability is the gap into which we can pour our love and support. Vanity blocks that whole process; the emptiness of self-love stops the natural flow of love from one person to another.

Yet people still need to be assertive in standing against injustice. The remaining five Beatitudes deal with this.

Blessed are those who hunger and thirst for righteousness, for they shall be satisfied.

Blessed are the merciful, for they shall obtain mercy.

Blessed are the pure in heart, for they shall see God.

Blessed are the peacemakers, for they shall be called sons of God.

Blessed are those who are persecuted for righteousness' sake, theirs is the kingdom of heaven.

While the first three describe those whose state of life makes them especially open to God, these last five Beatitudes deal with the moral challenges of life. They make it clear that people seeking justice and peace is another context in which God's kingdom is at work. But this hunger for righteousness has to be combined with the vulnerable attitude described in the first three Beatitudes. This is the Christian challenge: to seek justice with poverty of spirit, without anger and without vanity. God's power hungers and thirsts for peace and justice, but without rancour. It is unbelievably hard for human beings to keep faith with this way of living. But it can work. For example, in 1955 Rosa Parks simply refused to give up her bus seat to a white man, a meek act of justice that ignited the civil rights movement and changed the face of America. This is purity of heart in action, a hard-won quality that delights in doing the right thing. This is a happiness that knowingly ignores feeling good in order to follow the path of justice.

'YOU'RE DISRESPECTING ME'

In order to avoid right action becoming self-righteousness we need to distinguish self-respect from vanity. The use of the word respect has become so broad in its application that it now describes everything from government policy (the respect agenda) to an intense emotion (respect as part of love). Respect is now self-consciously fostered by communities as an antidote to vandalism and by companies as an essential ingredient in successful business leadership, while respect for human rights is a linchpin of political activity. If respect is now seen as necessary in so many areas of life, then the possibility of disrespect has also become more frequent. For example, a teenager was recently convicted of assault and sent to jail for violently attacking a fellow train passenger as they got off a crowded train. The teenager claimed that the other man 'disrespected me'. In cross examination, it emerged that this consisted of the other man pushing into him. Respect is now a highly charged word and people readily accuse other people of not showing it in many personal, social and political contexts.

To help us regain some balance in the use of this word, we can look at its original meaning. In Latin, *respicere* means to look at something with great intensity. But in the dictionary, 'to respect persons' is a corrupt act. It means to look closely at people's circumstances and then to show unfair partiality to somebody who is wealthy or influential.

That is why the statue outside a lawcourt has a blindfolded figure holding the scales of justice precisely to show that justice is not a respecter of persons. This means that the justice system must perform the following subtle task: it must promote respect *for* persons but not respect *of* persons. It must look closely at somebody's legal rights but not at their position in society.

If we apply that conclusion to self-respect then we will want to promote respect *for* self but not respect *of* self. In practice, this means knowing that I am entitled to justice but not to special treatment. Take the teenager who was shoved getting off the train: if the shove was intentional, then it was unjust; if it was simply the crush of the crowd, then he had no right to expect special treatment. In that situation, the man with a pure heart will give the benefit of the doubt to the crush of the crowd theory and will not allow his anger to cause him to attack another passenger in the name of justice. He will undoubtedly be the happier for it. So self-respect is a variation on self-awareness; we must be attentive to our inner world as well as to the actions of the people around us. A vain person takes every misunderstanding and every human error as a personal affront, as an attack upon their self-respect: 'You're disrespecting me' may simply be a vain way of saying 'I am angry that you made a mistake.' False self-respect attacks a fellow passenger who accidentally pushes us in the crowd. True self-respect is a black woman who refuses to give up her seat to a white man. The self-

185

awareness of a pure heart enables us to tell the difference between the two.

THE DECEIT OF VANITY

The greatest difference between vanity and the other demons, Cassian tells us, is that vanity redoubles its attacks when it is repulsed. So, for example, if we manage to restrain our eating, the thought of gluttony recedes. But when vanity is resisted it rushes back twice as strongly. This is because it accompanies the exercise of the virtues. When I stand up for justice, it makes think how impressive I am. When I am sober and chaste, it makes me complacent. 'Mingled with the virtues . . . it deceives the unthinking and the incautious', says Cassian. Jesus's parable of the Pharisee and the tax-collector illustrates this. In his prayer to God, the Pharisee lists all his virtues (and it's important that they are real virtues) and then thanks God that he is unlike ordinary people; he is special. The tax-collector simply asks God to have mercy on him, a sinner.

Cassian also describes a subtle form of vanity that we might call inverted vanity. This is when somebody describes how he could easily have acquired wealth and rank if he had persevered in his worldly ambitions, so now he boasts about what he has given up. This 'inflates him with a vain hope about uncertainties and fills him with boastful vanity about things he never possessed.' This is a monastic temptation but one that I have also come across among other people who have given themselves to the service of others. Once again, the demon of vanity clings to virtue and won't let go.

Cassian sees preaching as a moment when vanity is particularly likely to strike. For this reason, he wants monks to avoid becoming priests. He tells the amusing story of a monk who is overheard pretending to say Mass and preach on his own in his cell, the ultimate example of loving the sound of our own voice. Sometimes monks were (and still are) asked to become a priest by their abbot or by the local bishop. Cassian tells monks to avoid this and at the same time to avoid the flattering comments of lay women who will say how wonderful they are. He sums this up in a memorable phrase: 'a monk must by all means flee from women and bishops'.

The remedy is to remember to do nothing simply for fame; if we do something virtuous out of love of fame, we lose the merit of the virtue. In particular, he urges people to persevere steadily in what they have begun so that they may not find vanity creeping in; persevere because it is right not because it looks good. We must do what is right in the sight of God, not in the sight of human beings.

So when vanity is defeated, what virtue will

replace it? The opposite virtue of most of the demons is fairly obvious: temperance is the opposite of gluttony, chastity the opposite of lust and so on. Humility is the opposite of pride, not of vanity. Magnanimity is the virtue that defeats vanity. The word comes from the Latin *magnus animus* meaning literally a large mind or more colloquially a big heart. Bigheartedness is the opposite of vanity. The vain are rarely generous in the true sense; for example, they love in order to be loved back or they give a gift in order to be thanked. To experience genuine delight at giving something of ourselves to another person, we need to have a pure heart. The most common use of the word magnanimous nowadays is in sport where an athlete is described as 'magnanimous in defeat' if they praise the skill of the victor.

So if we return to our starting-point, the antidote to empty 'glory is a generous heart. This of course does not depend on having material wealth to give away; it depends on the interior attitude of love. The opposite of greed is liberality, as in giving away material goods. Vanity is a demon of the soul, however, and so is overcome by generosity in the soul not in the body. A magnanimous soul is one that can affirm the true worth of self and of other people without needing to make special claims for oneself.

In the Christian tradition, the Virgin Mary is seen as an icon of this quality of magnanimity that is the opposite of vanity. The song found on her lips after the Angel Gabriel has announced that she will give birth to Jesus illustrates this. Mary's song, the Magnificat, magnanimously affirms God's greatness and her own insignificance in the first two sentences.

My soul magnifies the Lord
and my spirit rejoices in God my saviour.
For he has regarded the low estate of his handmaiden.

Mary then goes on to make a startling claim:

For behold, henceforth all generations will call me blessed; for he who is mighty has done great things for me and holy is his name.

This sentence could be read as terrible vanity, but it is in fact the opposite. As in the Beatitudes, to be blessed is to be congratulated on the special action of God in your life. Mary affirms that future generations will congratulate her on God's work in her life. This is a magnanimous affirmation of God's work, not of her own efforts. The song goes on to say that through her 'God has helped his servant Israel.' Mary affirms that God is giving special treatment to all God's people. Earlier we saw that special treatment is the aim of somebody who is vain. And yet it is special treatment that God is offering his people. So what's the difference? The special treatment of vanity is this: a vain person demands to be considered special in order to hide their emptiness. By contrast, God's special treatment is a free gift that fills with love those who do not consider themselves special. Christian faith calls this special treatment God's grace. 'Hail Mary, full of grace', said the angel, and generations of Christians have repeated those words as an expression of what they too hope to receive.

The monastic tradition sees grace as an essential ingredient if the demons are to be truly and finally overcome. But the demon of pride, the last and most pernicious demon, keeps our hearts closed to this gift.

EIGHT THOUGHT:
Pride

Let the humble hear and rejoice
Psalm 34:2

If vanity is self-satisfaction then pride is self-importance. The two often go together, but it is quite possible to have one without the other. Somebody can be quietly self-satisfied without promoting themselves over others and similarly a person full of their own importance may readily admit to their own weaknesses. But pride is more serious than vanity because in the Christian tradition pride is seen as the root of all evil.

Before looking more closely at the sin of pride, however, we need to distinguish it from the pride that is considered virtuous. For example, people often speak of taking pride in their work. This is fine in so far as it means taking delight in a job well done and enjoying the recognition of others, but it is harmful if it means heightening somebody's sense of self-importance. The danger is that pride transforms self-esteem into self-importance.

If pride is always at the root of everything that goes wrong in our lives then we will not need to look too far to see it at work around us. Like vanity, pride is a subtle demon, which always finds socially acceptable modes of expression. So we can begin by looking at the currently acceptable ways in which people express their self-importance.

KEEPING BUSY

The first is to keep busy. The assumption is that important people are busy people and so if we are not busy then we are not important. Hence the question 'How are you?' is often met with the reply 'keeping busy' said with a rising, optimistic tone of voice. If we then followed up that response by saying 'Oh I'm sorry to hear that' the other person would think we had misunderstood. 'Being busy being important' is one manifestation of the busy culture.

This is not to condemn hard work, but it is a criticism of any activity that becomes so all-absorbing that it excludes other dimensions of life. Sometimes people who consider themselves busy are not working very hard at all; their self-designation as busy is a self-important way of covering up their laziness and keeping the rest of life at bay. Others who are working hard will often willingly take on an extra task because they do not consider themselves busy and have managed to keep life in perspective, working hard but also retaining boundaries. The busy culture is a frame of mind.

I came across my favourite example of the busy frame of mind when I went to preach at a Christmas carol service in Lewes gaol. Having passed through the rigorous security at the gates, I was escorted towards the hall. This was my first visit to the gaol, but as I walked down a corridor, a prisoner whom I had never met came up to me and said politely: 'I'm sorry I can't come to the service, Father, but I'm a bit busy this evening.' So the busy culture gets into prisons and it even gets into monasteries. Prisons and monasteries alike are designed to provide those who live there with a cell, a private place that is intended to remove any chance of being busy and self-important. Yet even this context can be subverted by the power of the keeping busy culture. So what is this culture that penetrates even prisons and monasteries?

People today find themselves driven to work harder and harder to pay the mortgage and sustain the consumer lifestyle that their families have come to expect as the source of their happiness. And then they need the package holiday to relieve the stress of the work, leading to more work to pay for the holiday. This is the core of the busy culture and it has been aptly described as a pleasure treadmill. Yet people do not want to step off the treadmill because there is only one thing worse than being busy and that is being not busy. People fear unemployment: they understandably fear the loss of income that comes from being out of work but they also fear the loss of importance. To become not busy is to become not important. So while there are many mixed motives for staying in the busy culture, one of them is pride.

KEEPING FRIENDS

The younger generation, those without mortgages, are less busy but have other ways of expressing their self-importance. The small circle of close friends is the key here. Happiness is achieved by having not only a circle of friends but also the technology that enables constant communication with them. Text messages and mobile phone calls, emails and social networking websites, these are essential parts of this friendship culture. As well as holding friends together, this personal communications technology has created a symbiotic relationship with the mass media and with the rock music industry. The music and the mass media are an integral part of the friendship group. Not all young people buy into all of this culture, but most young people subscribe to some of it, either consciously or unconsciously.

The 'keeping friends' culture as an expression of self-importance needs some explaining, as at first glance I seem to be demonising a highly valuable part of life. In itself, keeping friends is clearly good. It is the surrounding narrative that makes the current youth version of it both distinctive and potentially destructive. Or rather, it's the absence of any wider narrative that is the problem. The small group of close friends and immediate family now bears the whole weight of a young person's existence; no other groups have any continuing role. The individual only has a duty to generate happiness among their friends and family; the wider picture of life is simply that if everybody did this locally, then all that local happiness would generate a global experience of happiness. This is the generation that wants for nothing and so sees no need for any larger vision of life. This world is meaningful just as it is and there is no need to imagine any deep or ultimate significance.

The 'keeping friends' culture is about shared self-importance and it consciously excludes any wider importance offered by political, philosophical or religious visions. Indeed, such visions are often condemned nowadays as the sources of unhappiness in the world, while keeping friends is considered the one reliable source of happiness. Part of the reason for this is that students are educated in our schools to deconstruct all philosophies and stories; they are brought up with a suspicion of everything that lays claim to be the big story about life. But in the end, the main reason that they do not believe in such wider visions is because life is fine just as it is. Why can't everybody just be happy?

UNHAPPY DEATH

There is one disturbing fact that goes against the flow of this youthful view of happiness: in Britain and America, suicide rates among adults have been falling in recent decades, but suicide rates among teenagers have been rising. In his best-selling book *Bowling Alone*, Robert Putnam uses Figures from the US Public Health Service to put the point starkly: 'Americans born and raised in the 1970s and 1980s were three to four times more likely to commit suicide as people that age had been at mid-century.' So why are the most materially advantaged teenagers history has ever known killing themselves in such numbers? Depression plays a devastating role in this, as discussed in the earlier chapter on sadness. But that is shared with adults and does not explain the higher rate of suicide among teenagers.

The answer given by Putnam and others is social isolation. Declining numbers of young people take part in community clubs, join political parties or go to church. This is a generation that belongs to many loose groups but refuses to join any longer-term community. They will readily join in one-off events but their suspicion of institutions makes them wary of joining any kind of institution or club. They want to belong but they do not want to join. Studies in the USA suggest that many young people are spending long hours on their own. This means that if they cannot easily make friends, they are completely isolated because, apart from school, there are no formal structures to help them create relationships. Even if they can make friends, the pressure to have a successful set of relationships and love affairs is so intense that failure is unbearable. In a life that is only supported by relationships with a few friends, when those relationships fail, there is nowhere else to go. The growth of absentee parents for a whole host of reasons exacerbates this, as does the social mobility that puts grandparents at a distance.

Since they believe that close friends are the only really important people in life, young people carry the full weight of life with the support of just a few friends. This leads to a shared sense of self-importance within the group. Outside the group, or if the group breaks up, they are quite isolated. Paradoxically, the 'keeping friends' culture is one of the reasons for the growth in social isolation among the young.

BLESSED ARE THE NOT BUSY

We need to find ways to enable people to see their lives in a wider context that gives life a broader meaning. The two cultures of keeping busy and keeping friends give people a quick sense of self-importance that produces a high feel-good factor and are therefore the ideal expression of modern understandings of happiness. But to sustain feeling good by these means makes keeping busy and keeping friends into frenzied expressions of pride rather than free expressions of generosity and love.

We will need to be busy and we will want to have friends. But in the end our activity and our friends are gifts that we hold, not rights that we keep. We will find greater happiness in all that we do and in all our relationships if we approach them with a pure heart rather than a consumerised heart.

The way to do this is outlined by Jesus in the Beatitudes, to which we turn once again.

We see that Jesus is speaking about the people who do not participate in the 'being busy being important' culture: the poor in spirit, who know that they are unimportant; the meek, who are by definition not self-important; the peacemakers, who are modest; the pure in heart, who are unassuming. Jesus is describing an alternative culture where nobody is important and everybody has time for those who are insignificant. This is his kingdom, a place for those who do not fit into the busy culture. One of the core tasks of the Church is to be the shadow side of the 'being busy being important' culture: a community of people who are unimportant and yet who make everybody who comes feel significant. Each of us needs consciously to find ways to lay aside the tendency constantly to 'be busy being important'. We can do this by wasting time creatively, such as playing with our children or by giving time to those who at the material level give nothing back, such as visiting the sick or the lonely. We can do this by wasting time spiritually, spending time in meditation or reading spiritual books. We all know that such 'wasted time' makes us happier than any amount of 'being busy'. The reason is that these are acts of loving kindness that come from a pure heart.

As well as talking about those who are apparently unimportant, the Beatitudes also describe those who have broken relationships: those who mourn, those who are persecuted and those who are reviled. Even those who are merciful are part of the world of broken relationships in that they forgive those who have hurt them. These are people experiencing breakdowns in their relationships, where the circle of friends is either absent or has broken down. Jesus highlights those whose relationships have gone wrong. Such brokenness is another context where God is at work, another part of the kingdom of God. Just as wasting time creatively and spiritually counteracts the pride of busyness so befriending those who are not friends counteracts the pride of keeping friends. The community that Jesus and his disciples fostered was not simply a close-knit group of friends. It was a group that reached out beyond the normal social barriers to include large numbers of strangers. Strangers here means not only the socially excluded, the lepers and the tax-collectors, but also simply large numbers of people, so large that they are not all personally known to each other. This is what struck people about the early Christians, that they could be so generous to so many people. This is true community: a group that reaches beyond friendship. Such relationships are demanding and require both humility and generosity to overcome the pride that keeps us safely inside our own busy little worlds.

THE WAY PRIDE WORKS

We need a good understanding of pride and how it works to escape from it. Cassian describes how there are two kinds of pride, the pride of placing ourselves above other people (carnal pride) and the pride of placing ourselves above God (spiritual pride).

Carnal pride is the most common, and involves the monk rejecting the ordinary life of the community. Specifically, he considers himself above the rest of the community and is sometimes unkind to other monks. He is not content with the poverty of the monastery and tries to keep some private property. Even if he succeeds in taming some of the demons, his life is built on pride and so these virtuous efforts are all his own and will not endure. He is suspicious, loud and obstinate, is quick to anger and never apologises. Above all, he claims to be seeking the spiritual life while actually pursuing his own desires.

The carnally proud monk sounds a most unpleasant person to have around. But if we look carefully we can see that in fact most of us have something of the carnal monk about us, especially when we get caught up in 'being busy being important'. We need consciously to remind ourselves not to seek to have everything our own way, to restrain our suspicion of others and to distinguish our own desires from what is good for other people. In other words, we need consciously to pursue humility. At its worst, the busy culture is built on carnal pride and we can combat its negative effects by acknowledging our need for greater humility. This has nothing to do with humiliation, which is a cruel imposition of an inferior status. Humility is an honest approach to the reality of our own lives and acknowledges that we are not more important than other people. Those of us who carry responsibility for making decisions about other people still need to keep this in mind, even when our job requires us to judge another person. 'There but for the grace of God go I' is a saying that reminds us of a profound truth firstly about ourselves and then an increasingly forgotten truth that all the virtues are a gift of God. To combat the carnal pride of the busy culture we need to ask God to send us his grace.

The workings of spiritual pride are equally unattractive. Cassian tells the story of Lucifer as an example of somebody caught up in his own proud world to such an extent that he placed himself above God. Lucifer was the most beautiful and gifted of all the angels, but he thought that using those gifts at the service of his own wishes could make him happy. Classic theology says that God alone is self-sufficient, needing no will other than his own. Lucifer fell from grace because he started to believe that what is true of God alone was true of him. He thought that he didn't need any point of reference beyond himself in order to be happy. So God gave him what he wanted and left him to his own devices. Lucifer started to live by his own will and then discovered that he had a freedom capable of achieving everything except goodness and happiness. He had become a prisoner of his own will. That is the danger that lurks inside our contemporary youth culture: attractive, gifted people can become trapped inside their own world.

KEEPING FAITH

The song of Mary, the Magnificat, contains important insights about how to move beyond this world of carnal and spiritual pride. Following the lines that we looked at in the previous chapter, Mary says:

> God has scattered the proud in the imagination of their hearts,
> He has put down the mighty from their thrones,
> And exalted those of low degree.

In this song, Mary puts her finger on the source of pride: the imagination, the same source as greed. She continues:

> He has filled the hungry with good things,
> And the rich he has sent empty away.

The more important we think we are, the more we will consume, and if we feel unimportant the marketing tells us how we can buy our way to being important. Our imaginations are stirred up by consumer culture to want both more importance and more things.

    The Christian story offers us imaginative alternatives to the self-importance of greed and busyness. Through Mary's song, through the parables and through the challenge to our imagination that is the resurrection of Jesus, the Gospel invites us to imagine new ways to be free from destructive thoughts. Some people simply refuse to allow themselves to imagine a world in which people do not get angry, a world in which people are not greedy, a world where the proud are scattered. They are addicted to the current picture of how things are.

To imagine in this Gospel way is not to daydream. It is to be fully engaged body, heart and soul in working out new ways to live locally and globally. To exercise the imagination is not to say 'wouldn't it be nice if . . .' It is to be involved with other people in addressing creatively the issues facing our families, our communities and our countries. We can be inspired by Pope John Paul II imagining the collapse of Soviet communism when it looked so strong, by Leonard Cheshire imagining his own house as a place for those who could no longer look after themselves, by William Wilberforce imagining a world without slaves. If the proud are scattered in the imagination of their hearts, the humble are inspired to great achievements in the imagination of their pure hearts. Mary's humility does great things that the world's pride cannot imagine.

THE FINAL STEPS

At the beginning of this book, we looked at the Twelve Steps of Alcoholics Anonymous and saw in the middle four steps a description of self-awareness that enables us to recover our interior life and make it truly our own. The last five steps describe how, having seized hold of our self-awareness, we can then make a fundamental choice that enables us to reach out beyond ourselves. They read as follows:

8 *We made a list of all persons we had harmed, and became willing to make amends to them all.*

9 *We made direct amends to such people wherever possible, except when to do so would injure them or others.*

10 *We continued to take personal inventory and when we were wrong promptly admitted it.*

11 *We sought through prayer and meditation to improve our conscious contact with God as we understood Him, praying only for knowledge of His will for us and the power to carry that out.*

12 *Having had a spiritual awakening as the result of these steps, we tried to carry this message to alcoholics and to practise these principles in all our affairs.*

These steps describe the humility needed to move outside our own busy little worlds to embrace other people and to welcome the grace of God. They are repeated throughout life and not simply done once. As part of that process, people keep attending AA meetings where they create fellowship with friends and strangers alike. All this serves to illustrate what is missing from simply keeping busy and keeping friends. Imagining humble fellowship with strangers and God is what drives out pride and opens up the way to conquering all the demons of unhappiness.

DELIGHT

Cassian's teaching on the Eight Thoughts finds its completion in his conference *On Perfection*. He offers an image to describe spiritual perfection, with three stages of achieving purity of heart described as three reasons for being virtuous. At the first stage of spiritual growth, we want to be virtuous out of fear of being punished for doing wrong. This fear might be of human or divine punishment, or, I would add, fear of negative consequences. This could be characterised as virtue in response to fear of pain. At the second stage, we want to be virtuous out of hope of some reward. Again, the reward might be human or divine, and I would add possibly hope of some personal benefit. This could be described as virtue in response to hope of profit. But the final stage is to be virtuous out of love, love of doing the right thing, love of other people and ultimately love of God. Cassian compares these three to three kinds of relationship. Virtue in response to fear of pain is like the virtue of a slave who obeys a master. Virtue in response to hope of profit is like the virtue of an employee who wants wages. Virtue in response to love is like the virtue of a child who willingly responds to a parent.

Cassian recognises that nobody is completely perfect. Even those who act virtuously out of love cannot avoid 'those small sins that are committed by word, by thought, by ignorance, by forgetfulness, by necessity, by will and by surprise'. Realising that they themselves are dependent on God's compassion in their own sinfulness, the virtuous will have in particular the gift of compassion for those who are morally weak. While complete perfection is impossible, Cassian sincerely believes that we can diminish our willing embrace of the Eight Thoughts. We can make a fundamental choice to avoid them, so that while they may still influence us by forgetfulness or by surprise, our fundamental choice to reject them can remain firm. To make this choice consistently is the nearest we get to perfection; to make it not once and for all, but time and again. This choosing and choosing again is purity of heart.

The fruit of this is to take delight in the opposite of the demons: the virtues that we outlined at the start of our journey. Three virtues in the body: moderation, chaste love and generosity. Three virtues in the heart and mind: gentleness, gladness and spiritual awareness. Two virtues in the soul: magnanimity and humility. We can call these the Eight Virtues and they are the stepping-stones that we set out to find at the beginning of the book. To make a sincere choice to stand by these is purity of heart and to follow them as our path is sheer delight. To be a person filled with these virtues is to be a delightful person. But living the Eight Virtues is so much harder than embracing the Eight Thoughts and we know that our feet will often slip off these stepping-stones. With God's grace, however, we can persevere, we can be forgiven and we can start again each day with our feet firmly planted on the stepping-stones of virtue.

All too often, happiness is narrowed down to mean feeling good. There is of course nothing wrong with feeling good, but such a narrow definition leaves little room for the delight of virtue and the joy of grace. To find happiness, we need to broaden our definition so that feeling good is put into the wider context of doing good and knowing good. In this book, I have not offered any method for finding happiness because happiness is not an object to be grasped or lost; I have instead described finding happiness as a lifelong process that culminates in a happy death. This journey is one shared in different ways by both lay people and monks. The monastic stepping-stones are there to help us take delight in doing good and to have joy in knowing God's grace. As we take those steps we will indeed be on the road to finding happiness.

I began this book by reflecting on the need to find a solid understanding of happiness that is pure gold and not fool's gold. Embracing the Eight Thoughts is the fool's gold that offers happiness to the untrained eye. To live the Eight Virtues is the pure gold of happiness, a happiness that is robust, generous and everlasting.

Acknowledgements

Writing a second book really is ten times harder than writing the first one. So I want to thank the Weidenfeld & Nicolson staff who gave me the confidence to persevere. Firstly, I thank my original editor, Helen Garnon Williams, who, through motherhood and changing jobs, has never ceased to offer generous support and critical insight at every stage of the writing process. I thank Alan Samson who took over as editor during the final stages and continually endorsed my work while editing judiciously. Secondly, the success of *Finding Sanctuary* is the platform on which this book has been published. For her work in promoting that book, I thank Lisa Shakespeare who did so much beyond the call of duty to manage my encounters with the media, making them enjoyable and fruitful.

Next I want to thank my brethren, the monks of Worth Abbey. I gave most of these chapters to them as community talks and their critique has been of inestimable value. I thank in particular those who have shared with me their experience of facing the demons. I thank them all for their patience and their encouragement, not only as regards the text but also as regards how the Abbot writing a book affects our common life.

Finally, I want to acknowledge those out of whose learning I have built the foundations of this book. The Bible quotations are from the Revised Standard Version except for the Psalms which are from the New Jerusalem Bible. I thank the Liturgical Press, Collegeville, USA for permission to use their edition of *The Rule of St Benedict*. The writings of Dr Windy Driver have been a major influence on my understanding of Cognitive Behaviour Therapy for which I am grateful both personally and as an author. Above all, I thank Fr Columba Stewart of St John's Abbey, Collegeville, USA not only for his magisterial book *Cassian the Monk* but also for his friendship. He taught me how to take Cassian seriously not only in the modern world but also in my own life.

Bibliography

The works listed below have been particularly useful in the writing of this book and are highly recommended for further reading:

Cassian, J., *The Institutes*, trans. B. Ramsey, (The Newman Press, 2000)
—, *The Conferences*, trans. B. Ramsey, (The Newman Press, 1997)
Dryden, W. and Gordon, J., *Thinking Your Way to Happiness* (Sheldon Press, 1990)
Funk, M., *Thoughts Matter: The Practice of the Spiritual Life* (Continuum, 1998)
Gruber, M., *A Journey Back to Eden: My Life and Times among the Desert Fathers* (Orbis, 2002)
Hadot, P., *Philosophy as a Way of Life* (Blackwell, 1995)
McMahon, D., *Happiness: A History* (Grove Press, 2006)
Merton, T., *Cassian and the Fathers* (Cistercian Publications, 2005)
Miller, V., *Consuming Religion: Christian Faith and Practice in a Consumer Culture* (Continuum, 2003)
Savage, S. et al., *Making Sense of Generation Y: The World View of 15-25 Year-olds* (Church House Publications, 2006)
Stewart, C., *Cassian the Monk* (Oxford University Press, 1998)

Styron, W., *Darkness Visible* (Vintage, 2004)

Ward, B., *The Desert Fathers: Sayings of the Early Christian Monks* (Penguin, 2004)